theX blessing

UNVEILING A REDEMPTIVE STRATEGY FOR A MARKED GENERATION

Bishop Clarence E. McClendon

THOMAS NELSON PUBLISHERS®
Nashville

Published in Nashville, Tennessee, by Thomas Nelson, Inc.

Library of Congress Cataloging-in-Publication Data

McClendon, Clarence E.
   The x blessing : unveiling a redemptive strategy for a marked generation / Clarence E. McClendon.
     p. cm.
   Includes bibliographical references.
   ISBN 0-7852-6902-9
   1. Church work with young adults. 2. Generation X—Religious life. I. Title
   BV4446.M33 2000
   259'.25—dc21   99-047715

Printed in the United States of America
1 2 3 4 5 6 7 8 9 10 QPV 09 08 07 06 05 04 03 02 01 00

This book is dedicated to the loving memory of my father, the Reverend Doctor H. Levi McClendon, Jr., who was my first pastor, mentor, and a shining example of a faithful and integral man of God. He and my mother, Miriam, effectively instilled in me the fear and reverence of God along with the belief that God could use me to change my generation. I am extremely grateful to God for placing me in the hands of two parents who believed in me and who encouraged me that, with the help of my God, I could do or be anything.

contents

contents

acknowledgments

my sincere thanks and appreciation to:

• My entire family, who continue to release me to serve my generation.

• The Church of the Harvest staff and family, who faithfully undergird their Bishop and support the set vision of the House.

• Dr. Mark Hanby, Bishop Earl Paulk, and Bishop Paul S. Morton, Sr., men of God and spiritual patriarchs who have selflessly shared their wisdom, revelation, and experience with me.

• Numerous pastors and friends throughout North America who have granted me the privilege of ministering in the lives of the people of God.

acknowledgments

•Margie Waldo, for her skill and dedication in helping me sound intelligent in this book.

• Elder Derrick Noble and Marvin Johnson for simply finding time.

• To Thomas Nelson Publishers for partnering in this timely project. Special thanks to vice president Janet Thoma and managing editor Anne Trudel.

1

X marks the spot

there's something about being at thirty-five thousand feet. It provides a unique clarity and perspective. After weeks of grueling cross-country travel and a non-stop ministry schedule, I was grateful to once again find myself at that familiar higher altitude onboard an American Airlines flight heading home to Los Angeles. That day, like most days, had been filled with endless phone calls and the never-ending requests for decisions to be made. The in-flight meal service now completed, the only decision I still had to make was which CD would I fall asleep to: Fred Hammond, Lauryn Hill, Kirk Franklin, or Sting? That choice made (Sting), I settled back in my seat, closed my eyes, and began to drift away, rehearsing the events of the day.

My crusade team and I had been ministering at a conference in the Metroplex of Dallas-Fort Worth. We witnessed an extraordinary presence of the Lord that liberated thousands of men, women, and children as we opened the Word of God to those gathered. The Dallas crusade was our twelfth city in just nine weeks. That, in addition to the six services we preached each week at Church of the Harvest, set a rigorous yet wonderful pace. As I closed my eyes, an endless sea of faces remained before me.

I had slept for only a moment when I was suddenly awakened. The aircraft cabin lights were dimmed so that passengers could sleep uninterrupted. As I looked around, those near me were either asleep or engrossed in an array of magazines or books. As I laid my head back against the seat, the Lord began to replay the story of the patriarch Jacob blessing his grandsons Manasseh and Ephraim as recorded in the Old Testament book of Genesis (Chapter 48). As the narrative unfolded before me, it was as if I were a participant witnessing the event firsthand. Immediately I was caught up in what I was experiencing. Of course, I knew the story well, but I hadn't actually read it in months. What was going on? Why was I being drawn into this now?

As I continued to observe, Joseph carefully positioned his sons, Manasseh and Ephraim, before their grandfather, Jacob. They were prepared to receive his patriarchal blessing. Manasseh, the eldest, was at Joseph's left hand, facing his grandfather Jacob's right hand, and Ephraim was guided by Joseph's right hand, aligned with his grandfather's left hand. Joseph positioned Manasseh to receive the powerful right-hand blessing of the firstborn while Ephraim, the younger boy, stood by to receive what was left over. Jacob stretched his arms toward the boys, but at the last moment he crossed his arms, laying his right hand—the hand of blessing and authority—upon the younger boy, Ephraim, and his left hand of lesser endowment upon Manasseh. With this simple action, Jacob altered destiny. The younger son, the younger generation, rather than the firstborn, would now receive the benefits, honor, and blessing. At that instant I realized that when Jacob crossed his arms he formed an *X*, and the Lord spoke to me, saying, "Son, that is the X Blessing."

The X Blessing? "Lord, what do You mean?" I asked.

The Spirit of God said to me, "Son, the X Blessing is a flipping of grace and anointing, a crisscrossing of power and influence from the expected one to the unexpected one." I considered for a moment how the Church, by and large, has written off this generation—my generation—as rebellious, while the world has determined them to be unmotivated, uninterested, and lazy.

Much of the secular media, scholars, and psychologists have tagged these young people as "Generation X," meaning that they are a variable or an unknown. The "experts" freely admit that they don't know who they are or what to do with them.

The Spirit of the Lord continued speaking: "Son, consider the possibility that I have used the secular news media to alert the Church to My end-time battle plan and strategy. Their prophets were speaking while the majority of Mine remained silent. If the Church will adjust their thinking to understand that there is a blessing, rather than a curse, upon this generation they will find that there is a seed of deliverance in their midst that I am going to use to shake the nation. I am in the process of raising up and anointing a generation of people with a special dimension of grace. Although they have been maligned and misunderstood, I have My eye upon Generation X. This is the generation that I will use to spark revival in this nation."

I sat stunned. It seemed as though I had been swept up in this unfolding revelation for hours, while in reality only a few moments had passed. Oblivious to anything else, I recognized that I had been lowered into a vault of revelation—everything around me had suddenly faded to black, and I sensed my spirit and mind being expanded to carry the weight of this newfound understanding. Finally I unbuckled my seat belt and stood to remove my carry-on bag from the overhead compartment. I quickly found my Bible. I was eager to check my inspiration against the written account of this event in the Scripture.

With my schedule, finding blocks of time to study can be a challenge. Instead I rely upon a consistent diet of reading the Word of God, trusting the Holy Spirit to illuminate and bring to my remembrance those things that Jesus, by His Spirit, is speaking to me personally and directly. ("But the Helper, the Holy Spirit, whom the Father will send in My name, He will teach you all things, and bring to your remembrance all things that I said to you." John 14:26 NKJV.) Often after times of reading, praying, meditating, or simply resting, these moments of divine inspiration come upon me.

I was divinely agitated as I read and reread the words of Genesis 48; the images continued to jump off the page. "Lord, what am I supposed to do with this?" I asked. Instinctively I knew that something of my own destiny had been further focused for me on that flight to Los Angeles. For some reason, I had received and been entrusted with a twofold mandate: first, to alert a generation of people that, though they may not even recognize it yet, they have been prepared for the kingdom of God; and second, to awaken a generation, perhaps within the Church and *regardless of their chronological ages,* to the fact that they are part of a generation that God is preparing and positioning to use in this last hour and final day of harvest.

As we prepared to land in Los Angeles, I was astonished by all that had transpired in a few short hours. As I walked through the airport, my eyes focused upon the dozens of twenty- and thirty-somethings who crossed my path en route to baggage claim. I found myself silently repeating back to the Lord what He had declared to me: "Lord, these are *Your* seeds of deliverance, *Your* chosen ones—baggy jeans, purple hair, pierced eyebrows, and all. You have chosen them for such a time as this." Consumed with a sense of expectation, I looked forward to the following day's services at Church of the Harvest, eager to speak with my elders and staff about the commission we had received.

Church of the Harvest is located in the heart of Los Angeles's inner city on the corner of La Brea and Adams in the Crenshaw District. We are a rapidly growing multiethnic congregation of more than twelve thousand adults and children. Situated on approximately three acres and straddling one of the busiest intersections in West L.A., we face a daily exercise in creativity as we seek new ways to accommodate those desiring to receive from the Lord. In addition to our six weekly worship services and daily ministry programs, Church of the Harvest encompasses an international television and radio ministry that currently is accessible to 200 million households worldwide. Worship is high-octane in emphasis and style and is a nonnegotiable priority each time we open the doors. In this city, perhaps we are best known for our commitment to preaching the timely, eternal, and unadulterated Word of God as well as being a people among whom the miraculous flows.

That Sunday, with two services already under my belt, I was well into my message in our third service when I noticed Gerald. I didn't know that was his name until later, but he had my attention. Gerald looked to be in his mid-twenties and was painfully thin. Sitting next to him was a young woman with electric orange hair. As far as I knew, I had never seen either of them before. Tears were streaming down Gerald's face. As I preached I silently asked the Lord, "What do You say about him?"

"He's Mine," was the singular reply.

The message completed, we entered into the most important, and my favorite, portion of any service, the altar call. I said, "You're in this building today and the Word of God has ministered to your heart, but you have felt that God would never receive you and that the

Church would not accept you if they knew who you were or where you've been."

The more I spoke, the more intense the flow of tears that followed the lines of Gerald's emaciated face.

"Someone wrote you off; perhaps you have written yourself off. You've been on the run, but I say to you, your running days are over. I declare to you in the name of Jesus Christ that God is blessing the unexpected. It is an hour when God is changing the nature of people so that they might serve Him. You recognize today that God has a plan for your life and that Christ died so that you might be free. I want you to come to this altar, right here, right now."

Partially blinded by his tears, Gerald rose immediately from his seat and stumbled toward the front of the sanctuary. Within moments, dozens of other people had joined him, many of them teenagers and those in their twenties and early thirties—those whom the Church and the world had written off as "too far gone" or "unreachable." "The X Blessing," I whispered to myself.

I watched silently as the praise team sang and our altar workers prayed with these young men and women. Most were dressed in the gear of this generation: Tommy Hilfiger, FUBU, Nike. They wore spiked hair, bleached hair, hair in braids, no hair at all, tattoos, chains, and earrings. Some were crying, others reverently quiet as they prayed to receive Jesus Christ as Lord and Savior.

As I looked into their faces, the Holy Spirit welled up inside of me: "In the name of Jesus Christ, you are not less than anyone," I prophesied. "I break off of you the shackle of fear and intimidation. You are God's chosen children of destiny. You *will* rise up, and you *will* do His will, and you *will* call upon His name, and you *will* see His hand in your life. You *will* be blessed because it's time for this generation to do the will of God." The service erupted as people across the auditorium embraced the promise for themselves. When the service finally ended, I was exhausted but energized; we had two more services to go.

That night was our regularly scheduled healing and miracle service. Although we often flow in the miraculous, this service is intentionally structured for special focus upon those needing physical, spiritual, and emotional healing. During the miracle service the Spirit of God spoke through me, saying, "There is a young man present. You have been addicted to methamphetamines for the past two years, and you desperately want to be free from that bondage. If you will get to this altar right now, there is an anointing to break the chain that has held you captive and has nearly destroyed you."

To my amazement, the young man who responded

was Gerald. He had returned for the evening service. Rocking from foot to foot, he nervously explained that he was a Hollywood musician, a bass player, who had spent the past two years strung out on "meth," and more than anything he wanted to be free. As I stretched out my hand to place it on Gerald's head and pray, he was immediately enveloped by the power of the Holy Spirit. He began to shake violently; then there was absolute peace. Within a few moments Gerald was almost unrecognizable. Where darkness, fear, defeat, and a residue of death had surrounded this tortured young man, now hope, liberty, and a deposit of peace radiated from his face. "I was told that I would never amount to anything. But that's changed. I *know* it's changed. I *feel* that it has changed!" Gerald cried.

That night as I drove home, the declaration that the Lord had decreed on the Dallas flight flooded my spirit: "I am in the process of raising up and anointing a generation of people with a special dimension of grace. Although they have been maligned and misunderstood, I have My eye upon Generation X. This is the generation that I will use to spark revival in this nation." *People just like Gerald,* I thought.

"Holy Spirit, sow this promise into my spirit," I prayed. "Let me remain in a posture and position that allows me to hear all that You are saying about this generation. Teach me about the X Blessing and the assignment that You are releasing to those Kingdom men and women who will hear and obey Your voice at this time."

I knew that I had barely scratched the surface of this revelation called the X Blessing. As I pulled into the driveway, I simply asked the Lord, "What's next?"

2

nothing smells
worse than old fish

monday mornings are brutal for preachers. Experts say that preaching one hour is equivalent to working a manual eight-hour day. In that case, since I preach five one-and-a-half-hour services every Sunday, I put in more than a forty-hour workweek in just one day. I definitely agree with the experts! Most Mondays my body feels like it's been shoved through a meat grinder; that day was no exception.

In spite of my fatigue, thoughts of the X Blessing and the destiny of this generation marked by God captivated my thoughts. As I worshiped and turned my attention to the Word, the Holy Spirit reemphasized what God had told me the night of my flight to L.A.: although they are broadly misunderstood and don't even completely understand themselves, this generation

13

will be the ones whom the Father will lay His hand upon, and they will shake the very gates of hell.

As I considered writing about this X Blessing, some rolled their eyes and declared that there was no need for yet another book about this highly profiled generation called "X." I wholeheartedly agreed. This generation has been thoroughly dissected, defined, and analyzed. Global studies and opinions have offered conclusions spanning the spectrum from astute observation to the ridiculous. Fortunately, this is not another book *about* Generation X; rather, it is a prophetic call *to* a generation and a declaration from the heart of God to a people He has marked for His own purpose. It is a summons to the youth of a nation and an announcement of God's plan to transform and place His name upon a generation. It is a wake-up call to the nominal Church that the Kingdom of God truly is now at hand.

While this is not a book that seeks to define Generation X, we need some basic definition so that we begin our journey of the X Blessing revelation at the same place. Experts continue to disagree over the specific span of years that comprise Generation X; most agree, however, that Generation X is the largest generation in American history, comprising some seventy-five to eighty million young adults.[1] One out of every three Americans is included in this generation[2]; for our purposes they are those people born between approximately 1960 and 1982.

To generations who have gone before them, Generation X is an enigma and will surely remain so until outsiders, both individually and corporately, choose to take a closer look. They are not motivated by the familiar stimuli of earlier generations, and unlike the preceding baby-boom generation, which experienced transsocietal events like the Vietnam war, the civil rights movement, and Woodstock, Generation X has been bereft of any one defining moment or event to mobilize them; they are unaccustomed to moving en masse. Known to be fiercely independent, perhaps a common denominator among this populace is a far-reaching disdain for being labeled by any singular title or definition.

Sociologists consider the babies born as Generation X to be the least wanted of twentieth-century America; they comprise the first generation to come forth during experimentation with commercially produced birth-control pills. They also have the lowest collective self-esteem in living memory, and perhaps more than any previous generation, they truly are a product of their times; they embody the definition of contradiction. For example, Generation X has grown up in a world that offers more choices than ever before; yet in the midst of abundant choice and opportunity, they are also the most incarcerated generation in American history.[3] Within this generation there are more millionaires and yet more desperately poor per capita than among former generations,[4] and the gulf between the two extremes has never been so vast. Never before has there been a generation comprised of more immigrants, yet never has there been greater anti-immigrant activity within the same generation. They are a generation quick to recognize what is authentic, but painfully slow to exhibit true transparency to those outside of themselves.

Thomas Jefferson instructed our founding fathers that every generation is responsible to leave the next at least as well off as it had been. That responsibility has been rather consistently discharged until now. Economic experts suggest that Generation X may be the first since the Civil War whose members will not match or exceed their parents' wealth and economic success.[5] They personify a decline rather than an advance of a society's preeminence. They are the inheritors of scandalous political leadership, the recipients of a severely warped family infrastructure, and the products of an often visionless and chaotic education system. For the first time this century, educational skills are not surpassing or even equal to those of their predecessors, and to many this generation is considered to be "academically challenged."[6]

Generation X is the first generation of "latchkey kids" who arrived home from school each day to an empty house because their parents were away at work; from an early age they learned to be exceptionally independent.

Generation X is the thirteenth generation to inhabit American soil since the United States became a nation, and those who entertain theories based upon superstition suggest that this "unlucky" thirteenth generation is somehow cursed or marked for failure and disaster. These "cultural psychics" have predicted one thing correctly: this *is* a marked generation. However, they are not marked for failure or for demise. Instead, I am convinced that God Almighty Himself has designated this generation as a delivering generation; He has chosen them. In spite of widespread dysfunction, this generation is divinely equipped to fulfill an overarching purpose relating to God's Kingdom. God Himself has allowed them to pursue paths of independence and disconnection because He is the One who will call forth this generation and unify a fragmented mass for His purpose, in His time.

As a generation, they are being identified and set up to bring renewal to an often anemic and increasingly irrelevant Church, and they are poised to usher in the most expansive harvest of souls that this world has ever witnessed. They will shake nations who have been denied God's presence and power and who have been arrogantly and often ignorantly misdirected by national leadership, both spiritual and governmental. They will expose systems of religion and will literally appropriate and reverse entire industries and structures throughout our nation and around the world.

Throughout modern history there have been cycles of baby-boom generations followed by baby-bust generations. Following the baby boom of the late nineteenth century in America came the "Lost Generation." Strong similarities exist between the Lost Generation and Generation X. Equally interesting is the connection that buster generations, like Generation X, have with the introduction of new musical sounds within a society. It was in the midst of the Lost Generation that the new sound of jazz came of age. Another buster generation born in the thirties ushered in the completely new genre of music called rock and roll in the 1950s. The pattern continues with Generation X; they have birthed hip-hop and have been the catalyst for the evolution of the Hip-hop Nation that now permeates America.

It is important to note that these generational similarities extend beyond the secular and into the Church. Not only are there unique generational attributes that characterize secular society, there are distinctive generational endowments deposited within the Church. There is no question that Generation X has forever altered the music scene with the introduction of hip-hop and rap. Generation X is birthing another musical transformation, of equal if not greater impact, within the Church. A generational endowment has been entrusted to Generation X that enables them to move beyond the usual parameters of ecclesiastical worship. It is a sanctifying of what has been developed within them in response to their secular environment and upbringing. They have a divine ability to take on the independent posture necessary to achieve exceptional things in God. Most have been prepared to receive this anointing in the secular world, and it is the sum total of this preparation that God is now sanctifying and using for His plans and purposes.

As the Church, we are mandated to progress beyond what we have known. God has embedded within this generation a divine capacity for worship that pierces atmospheres and grants access to and the release of Kingdom truths and authority. The intensity of this kind of worship is a tool that allows for an exchange to be made, leaving at the feet of Christ deposits of mediocrity, religion, and "the norm," and retrieving gifts of authority, revelation, understanding, knowledge, anointing, and power that will enable them to take a generation by storm. (After all, the Bible clearly states that in regard to the Kingdom, "the violent take it by force"—Matt. 11:12 NKJV.) It is an expression that has less to do with style and more to do with posture and position. Those who are poised and purposed to hear and respond to the "right now" directives of the Holy Spirit will enter in. This atmosphere of penetrating worship is a generational endowment directly suited to bring about cultural transformation.

I contend that some of the greatest worshipers of this generation have yet to enter into relationship with Jesus Christ or to acknowledge that their gifting and anointing is heaven-sent. There are young men and women with incredible endowments of talent and ability who are leading large portions of this generation in worshiping any number of things other than Jesus Christ. Imagine what God could do in and through them if they were to exhibit a posture of partnership and surrender to Him. I am convinced that some of those who are greatly influencing the values of secular music and entertainment are marked for Kingdom purpose. This is a generation who have been entrusted with unprecedented gifts and avenues of communication. It is uninspired for us as believers not to recognize that this is a generation destined to communicate the attributes and activity of the Kingdom of God. Many young people are right now being prepared in the "hands on" schools of entertainment, music, and media, and they are developing expertise in a medium that allows global access for a revolutionary message and movement.

On the whole, this generation has yet to understand that they are chosen rather than cursed. Bombarded with daily reminders of their alleged inferiority, they are a generation under attack.

Mick is six feet, four inches tall, twenty-four years old, and a drummer by profession. His hair is purple and stands at attention around his head. His fingernails are painted metallic blue, and he has a one-eighth-inch plug pierced into his tongue. Mick favors sleeveless shirts that accentuate his buffed arms, which are covered with tattoos and present a visual evolution of his life thus far. The unmistakable aroma of patchouli precedes his entrance into any room. But while Mick's exterior demands attention, he is a gentle giant inside.

Recently Mick visited the studio of Jenae, an international photojournalist who attends our church. As they worked together he asked, "Why do I always have wrecked relationships?" As they talked, the Holy Spirit instructed Jenae to tell Mick how the Father sees him. "Mick, there's something that I need to tell you. I see all of this 'noise' on the outside of you, but I also see that you're gentle and kind and that you have great compassion for people, especially for the underdog. Do you realize that those are characteristics that God has placed within you?" As Jenae continued, Mick began to cry. All of his life he had wanted someone to notice him. The longer he went ignored, the wilder he made his appearance in hopes of attracting someone's attention. Finally someone had looked beyond the "shock" to see what was really there.

The Church is called to bring a prophetic, redemptive response to the hurts and pains of people's lives, not to further reinforce those pains by judgmentalism and criticism. In order to bring about that response, the Church must have a prophetic eye and an ability to see beyond *what is* toward *what is purposed to be*. This is absolutely essential if we are to reap a harvest in this present generation. The Scripture declares, "For God so loved the world that He gave His only begotten Son, that whoever believes in Him should not perish but have everlasting life" (John 3:16 NKJV). The reality is, God did not love the world He saw. You'll remember that by Genesis 6:6, God was repentant that He had ever created man. You see, He did not love the world that He saw, but He loved the world that He had purposed to be. As a matter of fact, God loved it so much that He refused to let what He saw remain the way it was.

I believe that through the gift of Generation X, God is both presenting the Church with an opportunity and supplying the Church with a constituency to fulfill its responsibility to be prophetic both in its response and in its vision. It will take a prophetic eye to look beyond the purple-haired mix of our city streets and see the purposed of God, but it must be done! And when it is done, wherever it is done, the Church will have within it a constituency of people who, in turn, will know from whence they came and will be able to spot others who, like themselves, are different inside than they appear on the outside.

Jesus made an interesting statement in the New Testament about God's Kingdom: "The kingdom of heaven is like a net which was thrown into the sea and gathered fish of every kind" (Matt. 13:47 RSV). In other words, when the rule of God is revealed, every imaginable kind of "fish" will be in the net. One of the deficiencies within the modern-day Church is that we continue to reproduce the same kind of fish. We tend to be very uncomfortable with gathering and drawing in fish that do not look, sound, or act like us.

I do not believe, as some do, that Jesus is returning on January 1, 2000 (and if you're reading this, you know that I'm right!). Nor do I think that the threshold of a new millennium is a signal for Jesus to immediately come again. Don't get me wrong—I absolutely believe in the Parousia, or the "catching away" of the Church and the imminent return of our Lord Jesus Christ. Theologians are correct in saying that every biblical prophecy preceding Christ's return has been fulfilled. The problem, however, is not with the *world*; it's with the *Church*.

The Bride needs much perfecting before she is worthy of Christ's return. Jesus said, "This gospel of the kingdom will be preached in all the world as a witness to all the nations, and then the end will come" (Matt. 24:14 NKJV). We have preached a gospel in most nations, but we have not preached the gospel of the Kingdom in all of those nations. We have preached the gospel of our religion and of our denominations; we've preached a gospel of "Churchanity" and even the gospel of salvation, but we have not preached the gospel of the Kingdom.

The Kingdom goes beyond salvation. The Greek word that is translated "kingdom" is the word *basileia,* which means, "the rule of God, the realm of God and the royalty of God."[7] The Kingdom of God has to do with the influence of the rule of Christ in the hearts of men. Therefore, wherever men go with the rule of Christ foremost in their hearts and thinking, the Kingdom of God goes. The Kingdom has to do with our perspective on things beyond church. The gospel of the Kingdom has to do with the rule of Christ coming not only into the hearts of men, but through that rule in the hearts of men, the dominion of Christ being exercised in the arenas and environments that we in the Church have perceived as secular. The gospel of the Kingdom, then, has to do with the exercise of Christ's dominion in the earth. It is basically the good news coming into every realm of life and society. Until it penetrates at this level, we have not completely manifested the gospel of the Kingdom.

I am convinced that because we have preached an incomplete gospel, we have continued to gather the same kind of fish. In many regards we have been an incestuous kingdom, having relationships only with people within our own family and continuing to reproduce after our own kind. What we produce often reflects the birth defects associated with inbreeding. We're called to be fishers of men, but because we're all the same kind of bait, we're catching the same kinds of fish. We look alike, we act alike, and we sound alike: "Hallelujah, brother. Praise the Lord!" God says, "I've got some other fish and they talk like this: 'Yo, yo, yo.' 'Whad up?' 'Straight.' 'Phat.'" These fish require a different kind of bait.

I am impressed that at this time in history, as we

prepare to reap the final harvest, God is positioning and equipping His children to be a fresh kind of bait to catch a new kind of fish. God is burdening some of us with an understanding that there is a generation, or a group of fish, to be caught who have not yet been effectively reached. They are fish waiting to come into the household of God, and they are ready to enter the Kingdom of God, but somebody has to cast bait that will get their attention.

I am convinced that God is preparing us to reap an unusual harvest. "The kingdom of heaven is like a net which was thrown into the sea and gathered fish of every kind." When the Kingdom of God is truly manifest, every kind of fish will be within the net. It is to this end that I believe the Spirit of God has begun to deal with me in saying, "Son, I want you to position yourself to reach My sons and daughters because it is time to catch a new breed of fish."

It's time for fresh fish in the Kingdom!

These observations invaded my thoughts that Monday morning. Though I was exhausted, I was beginning to understand God's vision for Generation X.

3

it's a spiritual thing:
jacob told, israel strengthened

having further considered this "marked generation," I expectantly returned to Genesis 48 and to my examination of the story of Jacob, Joseph, Manasseh, and Ephraim. As I began to read, I sensed that some keys to unlocking this generation's spiritual potential were hidden within this Old Testament narrative.

As the story unfolds, the patriarch Jacob and his sons have been living in their adopted land of Egypt for nearly seventeen years, ever since Jacob's favorite son, Joseph, rescued the family from starvation and demise. The text reads:

> Now it came to pass after these things that Joseph was told, "Indeed, your father is sick"; and he took with him his two sons, Manasseh and Ephraim.

> And *Jacob* was told, "Look, your son Joseph is coming to you"; and *Israel* strengthened himself and sat up on the bed.
>
> (Gen. 48:1–2 NKJV, italics mine)

As I waded into these first two verses, I was immediately intrigued. The Bible clearly states that it was *Jacob* who was told that his son and grandsons were on their way to visit him; however, the Word also records that it was *Israel* who strengthened himself to receive them. Now, Jacob and Israel are the same individual. You remember that God changed Jacob's name to Israel after he successfully wrestled the angel of God and found favor with Him: "Your name shall no longer be called Jacob, but Israel; for you have struggled with God and with men, and have prevailed" (Gen. 32:28 NKJV).

The name *Jacob* means "trickster" or "supplanter" and represents the natural or carnal man. The name literally means "to take by the heel" and is representative of a wrestling move where one grabs the heel of his opponent and flips him to gain a position of advantage. *Israel,* on the other hand, means "prince of God" and embodies the changed man, the covenant man, the man of anointing. When Jacob wrestled the angel, God changed his name from

Jacob, "the supplanter," to Israel, "the prince." (Thankfully, God is always about His business of changing tricksters into princes and transforming hucksters into men of God.) The essence of the observation is that what was about to transpire was not of the flesh but of the Spirit. It was purposed by the Spirit and could only be accomplished by the spiritual dimension of God's representative. What the name switch in the Genesis 48 narrative signified to me was that the events about to transpire were not of the flesh but of the Spirit.

When Jacob heard that Joseph and his two sons were coming to visit, the "anointing" rose up within him because what was about to happen was spiritual rather than natural. In other words, when the carnal man, Jacob, was informed that his grandsons, or literally his *destiny*, were en route, Israel, "the anointing," picked himself up to meet them. This verse reveals that the blessing that Jacob was about to bestow upon the next generation was not birthed or released from the flesh, but from the Spirit. Although Jacob's eyes were "dim with age" (Gen. 48:10 NKJV), the covenant man Israel was supernaturally strengthened by the Spirit to impart the blessing. Jacob, the last of the Old Testament patriarchs (for God is known as the God of Abraham, Isaac, and Jacob), was preparing to bless not only the generation after him, but also the generation that would follow his sons.

Unlike most families in North America today, the people of Israel understood the significance of blessing. When a father was about to leave this life, he would gather his children and grandchildren and pronounce a blessing upon them, passing on the patriarchal or covenant blessing from one generation to the next.

As we have seen, it was customary for the father to lay his *right hand*—the hand of strength, power, and anointing—upon the eldest son's head, signifying the transfer of blessing. The generational blessing was given to the firstborn son and provided a double portion of inheritance as well as the responsibility for carrying on the family name and covenant to the generations to come. Once given, a blessing could not be revoked. The Bible is very clear that the right hand was the hand of power through which blessing was to be transferred. The Bible also refers to the "right hand of God." Jesus is seated at the right hand of the Father because that is the hand of power (Heb. 10:12 NKJV).

Joseph knew that his father Jacob was about to die, so he took his sons to their grandfather's bedside to receive his blessing.

And Joseph took them both, Ephraim with his right hand toward Israel's left hand, and Manasseh with his left hand toward Israel's right hand, and brought them near him. Then Israel stretched out his right hand and laid it on Ephraim's head, who was the younger, and his left hand on Manasseh's head, guiding his hands knowingly, for Manasseh was the firstborn.

(Gen. 48:13–14 NKJV)

Joseph had carefully positioned his eldest son, Manasseh, so that he could receive the firstborn blessing from his grandfather. At the last moment, however, Jacob crossed his hands, upsetting the standard procedure. Israel intentionally reversed the established order of generational transfer when he released his blessing upon the younger son, Ephraim, rather than the older son, Manasseh.

While the established blessing of the firstborn was an ordinance of God, we find in Scripture that God occasionally goes around His own ordinance to work His will, and He circumvents His own statutes to manifest His blessing.

As I contemplated this story, I was once again reminded that the blessing of God does not always have to do with who shows up first, who's most qualified, or even who we think is most deserving. It has to do with whom God has purposed to use and destined to bless. God has a way of taking the unexpected and rejected things and turning them around in order to use them for His glory and to ultimately effect His purpose. That is good news for today's youth who have been looked upon with airs of suspicion and doubt by some of their elders. God looks at them and says, "I'm going to bypass My order and release a blessing upon this younger generation that will bewilder those who have gone before them."

The Bible further records that Israel was old and his vision was growing dim. Yet when he crossed his hands (making an X) and then placed them upon the boys' heads, he was "guiding his hands knowingly" (Gen. 48:14 NKJV). Joseph watched his father switch the established order and became angry; he was convinced that his father was making a profound mistake. But Israel firmly declared that not only was he aware of what he was doing, he was being led by the Holy Spirit. In crossing his hands, Israel initiated the X Blessing and transferred the anointing and blessing from the expected one, Manasseh, to the unexpected one, Ephraim. He gave the second born the firstborn blessing. Again the Spirit of God spoke to me and said, "Son, that is exactly what I'm doing today; I am crossing My hands and placing My blessing upon the unexpected generation."

We need to understand that God is in the process of progressing us, generation by generation. Each generation is supposed to exceed the previous generation in excelling in righteousness. Jesus said to His disciples, "Unless your righteousness exceeds the righteousness of the scribes and Pharisees, you will by no means enter the kingdom of heaven" (Matt. 5:20 NKJV). In other words, He said to the ones who were following Him, "Unless *your* righteousness, or your right standing with God, is in greater dimension than the generation or the religious order before you, you will in no way penetrate or manifest the Kingdom of God." Therefore, we see that God is constantly in the process, generation by generation, of pressing His people further into the Kingdom.

But when He finds a generation who becomes stagnant or too religious, He will do whatever is necessary to bring about renewal, awakening, and revival. Every once in awhile He unleashes the X Blessing, where He literally changes His own plan, breaks His own rules, alters His own flow, and does the unexpected.

As Jacob prepared to release his blessing, he rehearsed for this next generation the history of blessing that he had received from God throughout his lifetime:

Then Jacob said to Joseph: "God Almighty appeared to me at Luz in the land of Canaan and blessed me, and said to me, 'Behold, I will make you fruitful and multiply you, and I will make of you a multitude of people, and give this land to your descendants after you as an everlasting possession.'"

(Gen. 48:3–4 NKJV)

Here we see clearly that Jacob was the covenant-bearing father. The covenant began when God chose Jacob's grandfather, Abraham, by saying,

Get out of your country,
From your family
And from your father's house,
To a land that I will show you.
I will make you a great nation;
I will bless you
And make your name great;
And you shall be a blessing.
I will bless those who bless you,
And I will curse him who curses you;
And in you all the families of the earth shall be blessed.

(Gen. 12:1–3 NKJV)

The responsibility for perpetuating and carrying this covenant transferred from Abraham to his son, Isaac, and then from Isaac to his son, Jacob, also known as Israel. These are the three patriarchs.

Throughout Scripture, especially in the Old Testament, we can observe the use of "type and shadow," a principle of biblical interpretation wherein certain images, people, or times, while actual, factual, and historic, represent something beyond themselves. For example, *natural* Israel is always symbolic, or a "type," of *spiritual* Israel, which is the Church. So when we read of God's covenant, His relationship and His dealings with natural Israel, we can apply those same definitions and truths to spiritual Israel, which is representative of the Church.

The story of Jacob provides an extraordinary example of the use of type and shadow. Jacob was the third in the line of the patriarchs. There were three. Three is also the number of the Godhead or the Trinity—the Father, Son, and Holy Spirit. Jacob was third in succession, so he was a "type" or symbolic of the Holy Spirit. We can view Abraham as being representative of God the Father, through whom the initial covenant was established. Isaac is symbolic of the Son, offered as a sacrifice.

The covenant must come from the covenant-bearing

father because he is a "type" of God. The transfer of blessing that Jacob was releasing to his two grandsons was spiritual rather than natural. What Jacob was transferring to the two boys went far beyond tradition; it was a spiritual transaction that not only bequeathed them Israel's name, but also included the supernatural transfer of the Holy Spirit power that enabled them to fulfill their destiny. ("But you shall receive power when the Holy Spirit has come upon you: and you shall be my witnesses." Acts 1:8 RSV.)

Jacob continued his recitation of God's dealings with him:

> But as for me, when I came from Padan, Rachel died beside me in the land of Canaan on the way, when there was but a little distance to go to Ephrath; and I buried her there on the way to Ephrath (that is, Bethlehem).
>
> (Gen. 48:7 NKJV)

Jacob was rehearsing his journey from Luz to Ephrath. On the way to Ephrath, Rachel, the love of his life, died giving birth to their son Benjamin. The name *Benjamin* literally means "son of the right hand," or in other words, Benjamin was the son of blessing or the son of Jacob's strength. Rachel had first given birth to Jacob's favorite son, Joseph, the dreamer and great visionary. Jacob was letting Joseph and his grandsons know that before Rachel died, she produced or gave birth to Vision (Joseph) and Strength (Benjamin). Although Jacob had twelve sons, Benjamin and Joseph were most dear to him. This is significant because Jacob was communicating to his grandsons that they were the inheritors of a legacy of strength and vision, and that same blessing and anointing was being transferred to them.

As I consider this encounter of blessing between Jacob and his grandsons, it is evident that the truths represented in this story prophetically apply to Generation X. This emerging generation—labeled an enigma, a mystery, unmotivated, and rebellious—has been targeted by the God of eternity to fulfill His divine purpose. He is flipping His grace and transferring His anointing from the expected generation to the unexpected one. God is laying His hand upon the unanticipated and reversing the anointing so that the unexpected generation is the one that carries on the blessing. God has a way of taking people who other folks never thought would amount to anything and using them to shake cities, nations, and generations.

4

undoing the
"un" generation

For some time I have wrestled with the disturbing reality that we have a problem in America: the enemy is attacking the generation that is to produce revival. The problem isn't natural—it's spiritual and it's generational, and now is the time to deal with it. A casual observer could easily conclude that we have rebellious kids in America. We don't understand how a child can get a gun and kill another child because of a video game or a pair of tennis shoes. It's even more inconceivable to consider how children can amass an arsenal of automatic weapons, grenades, and home-made bombs in their homes and then unmercifully take an entire school campus hostage. Yet the problems that we are facing today really are not the problems of this generation. Our young people are the inheritors of a legacy of rebellion and disregard, and they are growing up in a world twice as cruel as any generation that has gone before them.

In spite of current trends, I do not believe that this is a rebellious generation. Rebellion presupposes knowledge and information. You cannot be rebellious unless you have some knowledge of what you are rebelling against. Our young people are not rebellious; they are uninformed. They are a generation without basic foundations—they are the "un" generation. Nevertheless, I am convinced that the generation of students and young people living on the planet right now is *the* generation. If there is going to be revival, if there is going to be a move of God, if America is ever going to change, we must look to our young men and women as a vital vehicle for that change.

In every generation problems arise and, if not dealt with, become increasingly intense. The Bible clearly reveals a generational digression that takes place:

There is a generation that curses its father,
And does not bless its mother.
There is a generation that is pure in its own eyes,
Yet is not washed from its filthiness.
There is a generation—oh, how lofty are their eyes!
And their eyelids are lifted up.

There is a generation whose teeth are like swords,
And whose fangs are like knives.

(Prov. 30:11–14 NKJV)

Scripture clearly reveals that there will be a generation of people who will lack the basic foundational elements of society that allow a culture to progress. Let me say in no uncertain terms, *we are living in that hour.* The Bible declares that in the last days there will be a generation who are disobedient to their parents, and then will come the "un" generation.

But know this, that in the last days perilous times will come: For men will be lovers of themselves, lovers of money, boasters, proud, blasphemers, disobedient to parents, *un*thankful, *un*holy, *un*loving, *un*forgiving, slanderers, without self-control, brutal, despisers of good, traitors, headstrong, haughty, lovers of pleasure rather than lovers of God.

(2 Tim. 3:1–4 NKJV, emphasis mine)

This generational digression in our modern culture began when a generation of people rebelled against the establishment, disregarded their parents, got high on drugs, and removed all restraint in regards to sex and relationships. These were the children of the 1960s.

They were the generation that cursed its father and did not bless its mother (Prov. 30:11). In what I believe was an honest but unilluminated quest for truth and purpose, these young people questioned and challenged the status quo, throwing off established value systems, removing old landmarks, and scrutinizing long-held moral and ethical mores. The wake-up call came when it became clear that this generation could not supply replacements for what it had thrown off, removed, and scrutinized. Ultimately, the 1960s became a generation *without reverence*.

And that generation that cursed its father and did not bless its mother gave way to " . . . a generation that was pure in its own eyes . . . " the children of the 1970s, the decade of "free love." Women took off their bras and burned them, streakers strutted their stuff, disco lived, and everyone was high on cocaine. It was the "me" generation. In the 1960s the landmarks were removed; subsequently, the next generation had no landmarks to return to and no concrete values to measure their behavior against. They did the next logical thing: they established their own definitions of right and wrong. Good and evil were now subjective determinations of the human perspective, dictated more by situation rather than by irrevocable truth. Suddenly, anything was OK— "Whatever feels good, do it." "It's your thang, do what you want to do" was the anthem of the day. They were "a generation pure in its own eyes, / Yet . . . not washed from its filthiness" (Prov. 30:12 NKJV)—a generation *without righteousness.*

In the 1970s the seeds sown in the 1960s were watered with a peculiar mixture of rebellion and ignorance that has produced the generation we have today. You see, it is one thing to be unclean, but another to be unclean when the context of cleanliness has been called into question altogether. When there is no accepted cultural standard or collective definition of what *clean* is, your definition is as good as mine—and both of us can be far from clean! It is in the shadow of this conclusion that I assert that our present generation is not a rebellious generation but an ignorant one. And I mean *ignorant* in the literal sense of the word, meaning "without knowledge." They lack the basic fundamental moral, ethical, and cultural foundations that generations before them took for granted.

Today's youth lack them because the legacy they received from the children of the 1960s and 1970s contained few, if any, absolutes. Regretfully, much of the Church remained asleep in the comfortable bed of religion while the answers a generation was crying for were in the message of the Kingdom of God.

"There is a generation—oh, how lofty are their

eyes! / And their eyelids are lifted up" (Prov. 30:13 NKJV). This verse describes the children of the eighties, the generation of immediate gratification and conspicuous consumption. In this generation, the eyes were on the prize: being "king of the hill" and "top of the heap" was the goal. Not only did we want it, but we wanted it *now* and we wanted someone to see us with it! After all, the whole point of *conspicuous* consumption was to be seen. In the 1980s the digression articulated in Proverbs 30 continued until the end totally justified the means. Who you were was less important than what you had (or had on!). Less important still was how you got it.

Here was a generation who were dealt the cards of dissonance. They inherited a legacy void of moral, ethical, and cultural absolutes, yet they were injected with the venom of lofty achievement and status. The correlation between morals and ethics and achievement and status were never clearly articulated to them. If you want to see true anger and violence develop within a culture or society, parade before them a preferred lifestyle of affluence and wealth and then create no ethical avenue of hope or opportunity by which to achieve it. At least two things will happen: first, they will use whatever means necessary to obtain what they have seen advertised; and second, they will feel as deserving of it as anyone without regard to the means by which they acquire it. In such an atmosphere the work ethic inevitably dissolves, and it seems obvious that becoming a millionaire through selling crack is just as good as getting a real job and earning it. The results, after all, are the same, or at least they look the same. And after all, it's the look that matters, right? The eighties were a generation *without regard*.

That was the prerequisite to what we have in the nineties, a generation *without remorse*. It begins with the *decline of reverence* and is further reduced to an *absence of righteousness,* then the complete *removal of regard,* and finally, *no remorse*. I believe that we are living in the generation described in Proverbs 30:14: "There is a generation whose teeth are like swords, / And whose fangs are like knives." Not only are kids killing today; they don't even know that they're doing is wrong.

I am amazed when anyone in our culture is surprised by this. This present generation is a generation who cut their teeth biting into an American dream that for them is really a nightmare. They have been told what they must be, but not given the cultural and social building blocks to become it. And while I endorse the need for education, education alone is not the answer. When will we realize that education merely enables people to more effectively execute what they already are—that it does not transform a person into what he must become to live successfully and peaceably with the world around them? If you educate an immoral man, you produce a brilliant philanderer; educate a violent man, and you get a more intelligent criminal; educate a generation without values, and you will produce sociopaths of genius proportions.

In the frustration of the nightmares this generation has inherited, and in the absence of real parameters and acceptable values, the children of the nineties are the natural by-product of previous generations. Their "teeth are like swords"—in speech and demeanor they seem brash and combative. Their "fangs are like knives"—when they encounter others, they seem to cut, dissect, and wound. This is their developed response to the environment they have inherited.

The *Engle v. Vitale* decision in 1962 found official prayer in public classrooms to be unconstitutional. It was here that the great modern digression we see in our public schools began. Before that piece of legislation, the major dilemmas facing American educators were gum chewing, running in the halls, smoking cigarettes in the lavatories, and excessive talking. Today that list includes students carrying handguns, knives, and bombs and selling and consuming illegal drugs. Our schools have become places where it's more important to have metal detectors than qualified teachers. Gun legislation and more laws are not the answer. We can pass every kind of law we can think of, and it won't change anything. If people can't get their hands on a gun, they will find something else to kill with—because the problem is not with what they're holding; the problem is with the hand that's holding it.

I'm thankful the situation is not hopeless. Jesus is Lord and the Word of God still works. I believe that our kids can be what they want to be, do what they want to do, and achieve whatever they want to achieve. God has put His best in them. I have no doubt that they can far exceed anything we're seeing today. As a matter of fact, they're supposed to. Revival is simply one generation exceeding the righteousness of the previous generation by stepping through an open door into another realm of the rule of Christ on earth. If we only do the same things our parents did, there will be no forward progress in the Kingdom of God on earth. We have some exceptionally gifted and good-hearted young people who have astounding potential, but they have to have somebody who believes in them enough to speak the truth and to teach them the Word of God.

Before she was saved, Tracie used to break down cocaine and prepare it for sale. Although she never used it herself (she stuck mainly to marijuana and mush-rooms), the stuff her group produced was top of the line.

"When a generation isn't taught to grow up, and common sense is not encouraged or instilled into a kid, they almost automatically fall into drinking, smoking weed, or doing drugs. It's like a rite of passage," Tracie recently told me.

Tracie's father is black and her mother is white, and until she was in junior high, she didn't realize that she was what society calls "mixed." Although she was raised with no religion at home, Tracie attended parochial school in Boston until her junior year in high school when she was expelled for questioning a nun about why they worshiped idols. She had "accidentally" stumbled upon the verse listed among the Ten Commandments that warns, "You shall not make for yourself a carved image . . . You shall not bow down to them nor serve them" (Ex. 20:4–5 NKJV). It was one of the first sincere questions Tracie had asked at school; nonetheless, Sister Mary Ellen went ballistic over her impudence and demanded that Tracie "learn only what she was taught and *never* question anything." There was no way Tracie was going to buy that, so she proceeded to cuss out Sister Mary Ellen. She was quickly removed from class and from the school, and as you can imagine, Tracie left with no love for religion or for God.

After graduating from public high school, Tracie went to Europe to visit a sister who worked in Scandinavia. From the moment she landed upon European soil, she wanted nothing more than to come home to America, but she had no money for a return ticket. She complained unmercifully until her sister and friends were fed up and left her pouting in her room while they traveled to Denmark and Norway.

All by herself, Tracie was a wreck. Late one night, she flipped through her CDs and chose one by the Winans that she had never listened to before; someone had given it to her before she left the States. Alone in a country where she knew no one and couldn't speak the language, Tracie listened intently as the Winans sang. They were singing about Jesus—she knew Jesus from school, but this Jesus was different. She understood Him. That night she prayed, "God, I don't really know You and I don't know how to get to You, but I want what those guys on the CD are talking about. If you will just get me back home, I promise that I will find You." Her sister soon returned from her trip and seven days later, Tracie was back in Boston.

Tracie was serious about finding God, so the first place she visited was the Catholic church because it was familiar to her. After sitting through Mass, however, she knew that she hadn't found the answer yet. Her next stop was a Jehovah's Witness hall, and for several weeks she tried to find God there. Dissatisfied, Tracie explained her dilemma to an old friend who immediately knew the answer to her quest: witchcraft! She taught Tracie how to light candles and recite various incantations depending upon her need; together they sent curses across the universe. Then one day, while sitting on her roof lighting candles, Tracie stopped and said, "What am I doing? This is absolutely ridiculous. I must be out of my mind. God, this cannot be You!"

In the midst of her search for God, Tracie read *The Autobiography of Malcolm X*. She liked Malcolm and could relate to him, so she figured that the Nation of Islam must be where God hung out. For months she read books and attended meetings, loving the structure and discipline as well as the black pride that the Nation of Islam instilled within her. Over time, however, she sank into deep depression. While she enjoyed the academic challenge of the religion, she experienced no joy. "Islam gave me plenty of information, but there was no power," she remembers, and she began to drift away.

Throughout her exodus Tracie stayed in touch with her friend Cassandra, who had moved from Boston to Los Angeles. Cassandra kept telling Tracie about a church she was attending and how she was learning about Jesus and being taught the Word of God. As

Tracie listened, she could tell that there was something different about Cassandra. She had been almost neurotic before, but now she sounded peaceful and genuinely excited about the direction her life was headed. For months Cassandra begged Tracie to visit L.A. so she could take her to this "awesome church." Finally Tracie agreed and arranged to visit Southern California.

Tracie and Cassandra attended our midweek service at Church of the Harvest. They were back again Sunday morning and Sunday evening. The following Wednesday, Tracie gave her heart to the Lord. She returned to Boston just long enough to pack up her apartment and return to L.A.; she had finally found the God she had been looking for.

Tracie recently celebrated her seventh anniversary of being in relationship with Christ. Today she is the proud mother of two toddlers and works part-time in the public-relations industry. No matter where she goes, people are immediately drawn to her and want to know, "What is it about you?" She's quick to tell them about Jesus. Tracie has an insatiable hunger for the Word of God, and her great love is ministering to kids on the streets; she has such compassion for those whose lives revolve around buying, selling, and using drugs because that once was her world.

Tracie has befriended a young drug dealer named

David. He likes Tracie and endearingly calls her the "church lady." When they first met, David told her, "If I wasn't sinning, then maybe I'd talk to God—but I've got to do what I've got to do, you know. I really can't be your friend because of what I do. I mean, God would never hang with that."

Tracie assured him that they could be friends, and when she first learned his name, she nearly fell over. "David! What a powerful name," she said. "Do you have any idea who you are named after? Let me tell you." She told him the story of his namesake, a mighty biblical warrior who grew up to become king.

Now whenever Tracie stops in David's neighborhood, he is quick to greet her and to offer her protection. Tracie is convinced that David is a "marked man." "It's just a matter of time, because God has a phenomenal plan for this young man's life," she says. "He's an exceptional businessman and leader. Even though his business is on the streets, he knows how to recruit and train new 'employees,' he understands how to 'raise money,' and he is absolutely without fear. We need him working with us in the Kingdom of God! You watch, he's a marked man for the Kingdom."

5

the coming baptism: a baptism of repentance

among those who are hearing the voice of God as it relates to what time it is, there is a corporate understanding that it is absolutely not "business as usual." Within the Kingdom of God today we are in the midst of a dispensation, or set period of time, when God is moving upon His people in an unprecedented way. God is releasing something new upon His Church that is not exclusive to any one church or to any one people; rather, it is a pervasive move throughout the body of Christ wherever people are naming the name of Jesus and are willing to move into new arenas of dominion, authority, and understanding in Him.

In this season God is releasing a *baptism of repentance* upon His Church. Often when we hear the word *repent*, we automatically think of salvation, of weeping at altars and somebody giving his or her heart to Jesus Christ. Repentance certainly does lead to salvation, and salvation is absolutely necessary. Repentance, however, is not for salvation only. We are in constant need of the baptism of repentance *after* salvation if we are to progress in our relationship with Christ.

To understand the framework for this baptism of repentance, let's look at the book of Acts:

> Repent therefore and be converted, that your sins may be blotted out, so that times of refreshing may come from the presence of the Lord, and that He may send Jesus Christ, who was preached to you before, whom heaven must receive until the times of restoration of all things.
>
> (Acts 3:19–21 NKJV)

In verse 21, the New King James Version records the word *restoration,* but the King James Version reads *restitution,* which is a more accurate translation. *Restoration* means "a putting back," but *restitution* means "a giving back to the rightful owner of something that has been lost or taken away." It is a return to a former condition. So Peter is saying that God is going to send Jesus Christ, but the heavens must hold Him until those things that have been lost or taken away are given back to their rightful owner. He must be held until the Kingdom of God is more fully revealed and manifested through God's people. This will happen when we are moving in such power and authority that we indeed are possessing and restoring things on earth back to their rightful owner. As this occurs, the rule of God will be more and more manifest in the earth according to God's original intent before the Fall.

The gospel of Luke records how this restitution is made possible:

> While Annas and Caiaphas were high priests, the word of God came to John the son of Zacharias in the wilderness. And he went into all the region around the Jordan, preaching a baptism of repentance for the remission of sins.
>
> (Luke 3:2–3 NKJV)

As I read this recently, the Spirit of God said to me, "Clarence, I am releasing a mighty baptism of repentance upon the Church; it is John's baptism." After extensive study, I came to understand that John's baptism was not necessarily water baptism. John's baptism was one of repentance. John did not come preaching, "Be saved!" He came preaching, "Repent, for the kingdom of heaven is at hand." This baptism of repentance is a supernatural ability given by the Holy Spirit to those who will hear and receive the Word of God, which enables them beyond their human ability to release old ideas and traditions and to be open to what is coming next. In John's day it was an openness to receive the manifestation of the person of the life-giving Christ in the context of a lifeless religious system.

Today, where this baptism of repentance is released and received, I believe we will witness a modern-day continuation of the book of Acts. It will be as if the darkness and the digression of the last two thousand years of church sectarianism, denominationalism, and division never occurred. There will come a restoring in the hearts and the minds of the people of God that same Kingdom perspective that was resident in the early church. Because the early church had no Western church history to "unlearn," they were able to quickly grasp what now appear to us to be revolutionary directives and radical inspirations. In reality, it was the same Spirit of God that we have, supplying them with answers and solutions for the cries and the needs of their culture and society. Equipped with this baptism of repentance and Holy Spirit boldness, they were able to shake off the dust of incarcerating tradition and boldly go where men had not gone before, not just geographically, but spiritually, culturally, and socially.

This baptism of repentance is not something that is going to happen only within Baptist, Church of God in Christ, Foursquare, Catholic, or Presbyterian churches; it is going to happen within every denomination and outside of denominations. There will be a people of God, regardless of denomination or ecclesiastical fellowship, who will receive this baptism, and with it a supernatural ability and grace to consider and embrace what God is doing next.

Matthew provides further insight: "In those days John the Baptist came preaching in the wilderness of Judea, and saying, 'Repent, for the kingdom of heaven is at hand!'" (Matt. 3:1–2 NKJV) The word *repent* comes from the Greek word *metanoeo,* which derives from *meta,* meaning "after," and *noeo,* meaning "to think."[1] In other words, *repent* literally means to "think again." John came literally saying, "Think again, for the kingdom of heaven is at hand." It is time to rethink how we "do church" and to realign our Christianity more closely to what is revealed in Scripture about the Kingdom of God.

John came shaking the traditions and the religious ideals of the nation. We can expect some of the same results today. This baptism of repentance that God is releasing upon His Church is meant to shake us loose from our traditions, religious perspectives, and dogmas that have reduced the Church's power and, in many cases, kept us separated and fighting. God is saying, "Wait a minute! I did not leave nine hundred churches on earth; I left one Church. And I gave one Word and one Spirit." God is releasing upon His Church today an anointing that is raising people above the walls of denominational division and petty isolationism.

John the Baptist came with a fresh anointing that freed people to receive whatever God would do next. In another moment of divine insight, the Spirit of the Lord said to me, "Son, I am releasing a baptism of repentance upon My Church. Expect radical, sweeping changes to occur within My body and for old ideas, superstitions, and separations to be pulled down. In addition, those whom I am working in are going to know and recognize one another."

In other words, there will be believers within every denomination and beyond who will receive the baptism of repentance. We will recognize one another across denominational lines and geographic borders, and we will sense kindred spirits across ethnicity, gender, and generations. The fruit of this baptism will include an obvious lack of doctrinal entrenchment (without compromising doctrinal integrity) as well as an absence of narrow-minded fighting.

Much of the Church has majored in minors, and we

have excelled in the insignificant. We must begin to major in what God is interested in. Jesus said, "If I be lifted up from the earth, I will draw all men unto me" (John 12:32 NKJV). This is what God is beginning to rain down upon His Church, and I don't know about you, but I want it. Forget the drama, forget the separations, forget the mess—I want a move of God!

The Spirit of God also said to me, "Clarence, do not be surprised, for I will change your mind overnight. You will go to sleep thinking one thing and wake up to My Spirit revealing fresh truth to you about Jesus, and your mind will be changed in an instant." Therefore, I believe that God will change our minds to such a degree that, when we see Jesus for who He really is, when we understand the Kingdom of God, and when we see the Church for what it is meant to be, we are going to wonder how we could have been so far off. In many regards the modern Church bears little resemblance to the Church that Jesus left; however, the Spirit of God is jump-starting His Church into a proper alignment, where His Spirit will be free to move within and among His people.

"And he went into all the region around the Jordan, preaching a baptism of repentance for the remission of sins" (Luke 3:3 NKJV). The word *baptism* comes from the Greek *baptizo*, which means "to immerse or to be swallowed up in."[2] Again, the word *repentance* means "to think again, to reexamine, or to change direction."[3] So John came preaching, "Think again so that you can change your direction."

Such an immersion in repentance creates an ability to recognize and to embrace God's progressive anointings and manifestation. We all have come across people who are so steeped in religion, tradition, or their own ideas that they are unable to receive truth or embrace anything new. These are often people who have not yet been immersed in the spirit of repentance and therefore lack the supernatural ability that enables one to say "Yes" to God whenever He shows up.

It is critical that we understand that we are not meant to live by only what God *has said*. His Word instructs that we are to live by every word that He *says*. "Man shall . . . live . . . by every word that *proceedeth* from the mouth of God" (Matt. 4:4 NKJV, emphasis mine). The verse doesn't say "proceeded"—it is not something of the past—but "proceedeth"—those declarations and directives that are coming forth from His mouth right now in line with the written revelation of His Word. God's Word is a proceeding Word—it is always coming forth, and it is always fresh and on time; it is never stagnant, late, or irrelevant.

I appreciate what Dr. Mark Hanby teaches about

"proceeding words." He says that most of us would have sacrificed and killed the boy Isaac. We would have picked up that knife and murdered him because God said so. But the same God who said, "Kill Isaac" also said, "Don't kill the boy." We have to be so sensitive to the Spirit of God that we can stop our hand between the raising of the blade and the slicing of the sacrifice. God may say, "Go this way" today and He may say, "Go that way" tomorrow. Which one did He say? He said both. We have to be able to change directions with God. How many of us have "killed" things because God told us to and we didn't hear the next word that told us not to? *Ouch.* The baptism of repentance enables us to rapidly switch gears and accurately change directions with God.

It is my experience that religion makes people mean, and the longer we stay in it, the nastier we get. God is unleashing upon His body a grace and an ability to step out of traditions and dogmas that are killing us and stopping the flow of His power. That's why it is so important that we understand that we do not preach a religion, but we preach Jesus Christ. We're not talking about joining a church; we're talking about getting saved and coming to know that Jesus Christ truly loves us. When the Church begins to take on the true nature of Christ, we will not have to ask people to get saved. The day is coming when, in churches across America, people will stand outside the doors, listening and wanting to get in. When the doors open and the people pour out, they're going to say, "Listen, I wasn't able to get into the church today, but will you tell me how to be saved? Will you tell me about the love of God?" It is going to happen in this nation because God is unleashing His power upon people who will receive it.

We must leave behind our layers of tradition that hold us hostage. We must lose our carnal minds and appropriate His mind. We must not be surprised when we start seeing things differently. Our minds are going to be changed about things that we thought we clearly understood, and those people whom the Church has condemned to hell or completely disregarded are going to start coming to the forefront of our vision.

I submit to you that the reason much of America and much of Generation X have rejected Christ is because it has not yet met Him. With all of our preachers and all of our gospel TV exposure, the vast majority of our nation has yet to meet Christ. They've met our religion, our tradition, and our ministries, but they have not really met our Christ. It is time that America met Jesus Christ. There is an entire generation of people we cannot reach if we do not alter our perception of them as well as our perception of the Church and the Kingdom of God.

Our ministry team met JC at L.A. International Airport as we arrived home from New York City. We had experienced remarkable ministry as well as an unusual release of the supernatural in New York, and we were exhausted yet content as we boarded our flight for the West Coast. Back home at LAX, we gathered to await our luggage. In the midst of the growing crowd I noticed JC. He was in his mid-twenties and was a baggage handler for Delta Airlines. He, too, was eager for our luggage to arrive so that he could finish his shift and head home. As I watched this young man, I saw a distinct sadness that hung upon him. Finally the luggage carousel jerked into motion, and my team and I positioned ourselves to retrieve our baggage. As I looked to my right, there was JC, so I simply asked, "How ya doing?"

"Uh, yeah, I'm fine . . . fine," he mumbled.

"Really?" I asked. That question unlocked a brief but intense story.

Three days earlier JC's nine-year-old nephew had been killed while playing in his front yard, the victim of a drive-by shooting. His death had devastated JC's family. "He was so smart," JC remembered. "Man, he knew his way around a computer. He always schooled me when we played games." JC's voice grew soft. "And he loved music. He was gonna be a drummer. He was just learning to play the drums at school, and he was always practicing. We could hear him tappin' his sticks on the wall in his room, figuring out new rhythms. He was such a good kid. It's just a shame."

My heart twisted as images of my own three kids filled my mind. We talked a moment and I offered JC any help we could provide. He thanked us and we parted ways.

A few days later one of my staff received a phone call from JC. He had randomly dialed an extension once inside our phone system at the office. "Church of the Harvest, how may I help you?" the man from our staff answered the phone.

"Uh, yes, sir. Um, I just have one question," JC fumbled.

"Yes?" one of my men asked.

"Is your bishop for real?"

"Well, yes, sir, he is for real. Why do you ask?"

JC went on to explain that he had met us at LAX and that when he needed hope and a kind word, we were there to talk with him. "I meet famous people all the time—I mean it's L.A., you know? Musicians, actors, church people, and government types. But your bishop is the only one who asked about me; he inquired about my soul and about my well-being. I haven't been to church in years—there wasn't anything there for me—but I think I'd like to be a part of your church."

Now JC is a regular participant in our worship services simply because someone took the time to ask a hurting young man how he was and to show him Jesus in a way that made sense to Him.

6

a seed of deliverance

throughout history we can see a pattern of God "hiding" His deliverers until it is time for them to be revealed. When the spirit of the day seeks to emasculate or destroy His seed of deliverance, God hides His delivering people. I submit to you that in a time where the spirit of death has been roaming through the Church and where there has been sterilization by reason of religion, at a time when the Church has been taking "religious birth control" and has in many sectors become stagnant in sanctimony and ceremony, God has by His divine plan hidden a generation of deliverers outside the Church. We look at them and call them "worldly, secular, unchurched, and unreachable," but God looks at them and calls them, "Mine!"

As I sat and considered this, I realized that I had come full circle and was once again thinking of Genesis 48 and the story of Jacob, Joseph, his sons Ephraim and Manasseh, the X Blessing, and the compelling declaration the Lord unveiled to me while flying from Dallas: "If the Church will adjust their thinking to understand that there is a blessing, rather than a curse, upon this generation, they will find that there is a seed of deliverance in their midst that I am going to use to shake the nation."

Today we are confronting the same spirit that moved upon Pharaoh in the day of Moses and that moved upon Herod at the birth of Jesus. We are confronting a spirit that wants to steal the seed of revival and deliverance. It's interesting to note that the two major tools of deliverance recorded in the Bible— Moses and Jesus—God called out of Egypt. Remember that *natural* Israel is always symbolic of, or a type of, *spiritual* Israel, which is the Church. Egypt, on the other hand, is a type or symbol of the secular world and its systems. It represents paganism and carnality. Therefore, when we speak of being called "out of Egypt" or "raised in Egypt," we are referring to being called out of the world and its systems or being trained in secular or nonchurch settings and arenas.

Until today, never has there been a generation of people who are under such diabolical attack. We shouldn't be surprised, however, because the enemy has a history of attempting to steal and "snuff out" God's seed of deliverance. You'll remember that when Jesus was born, there was a star in the East that identified the location of His birthplace. Wise men sought Him, and upon arriving in Jerusalem they asked, "Where is He who has been born King of the Jews? For we have seen His star in the East and have come to worship Him" (Matt. 2:2 NKJV).

Before departing the city, they were commissioned by King Herod to find "the young Child, and when you have found Him, bring back word to me, that I may come and worship Him also" (Matt. 2:8 NKJV). But Herod wanted to kill Jesus; he knew that He was ordained to be the Deliverer. The wise men, after receiving divine warning in a dream that they should depart for their country via an alternate route, double-crossed Herod. When Herod realized that the wise men were not returning with Jesus, he had all the babies in the region killed in a vain attempt to destroy the "seed of deliverance."

But God knew how to hide Jesus. An angel of the Lord appeared to Jesus' father, Joseph, saying,

"Arise, take the young Child and His mother, flee to Egypt, and stay there until I bring you word; for Herod will seek the young Child to destroy Him."

When he arose, he took the young Child and His
mother by night and departed for Egypt, and was
there until the death of Herod, that it might be fulfilled which was spoken by the Lord through the
prophet, saying, "Out of Egypt I called My Son."

(Matt. 2:13–15 NKJV)

God directed Joseph to take Mary and Jesus into
Egypt, into "the world," in order to hide Him until the
stage was set for His return. When Herod was dead,
the angel of the Lord returned to Joseph and said,
"Arise, take the young Child and His mother, and go to
the land of Israel, for those who sought the young
Child's life are dead" (Matt. 2:20 NKJV).

Jesus was born, and Herod sought His destruction
because he recognized that a Seed of deliverance was
rising that would literally shake the nation and over-
turn his kingdom. He tried in desperation to kill that
Seed before it could grow into fruition. Meanwhile, the
angel of the Lord countered Herod's plans by directing
Joseph to safety. While Herod searched Israel for the
"Seed," Jesus was hanging out in Egypt, because God
knew that Herod would never look in Egypt for a Seed
of deliverance! No, he was looking in First Baptist,
First Methodist, First Presbyterian . . . He was looking
in *the Church* for the deliverer; he never considered

looking in the "world." After Herod's death, the angel of the Lord directed Joseph to return to Israel.

I submit to you that we have a generation that has been hiding out in the world unrecognized because the Church has not been ready to receive them. The Spirit of the Lord has instructed me, saying, "Clarence, I have been hiding some of My best seed in 'Egypt.' I've kept them hidden in the 'world' and in its systems because there have been people in My Church who have sought to kill them."

What a staggering thought! Many in the Church have not been ready to receive the sons and daughters God is bringing "out of Egypt," because we would have killed their spirit and their vision before they ever got established in His Church. Our religion would extinguish the life right out of them by telling them, "Turn your hat around, pull up your saggin' pants, pull that hem down, cover that tattoo, stop listening to that music."

But God says, "I don't want you messing with them; you're not ready for these yet. I've been hiding them in 'Egypt,' preparing them to fulfill My plan and purpose. Son, here is what I want you to do: I want you to lift up your voice and call them out of 'Egypt.' Tell them that the spirit who sought to kill them is dead."

Recently while on the road I had the opportunity

to talk with a young man who is a prominent drug dealer in his city. Dressed in my traveling gear, I looked like anything but a television preacher. I'm sure that had the police seen me talking with this guy, they would have assumed that we were in cahoots. He began to explain to me that he had no choice of careers. "I have no other way to make it in this world," he said. "I haven't been left with anything else: no education, no job experience. Nobody will hire me. All I've got is the streets. So I learned to do in the streets what I could do to make it."

I sat there thinking, *What do I say to this young man? I have nothing to say to him.* Then the wisdom of God came to me and I said, "There's one thing that you can do. You can sell just about anything to anybody, and that's a real skill. You definitely have the power of persuasion—you're selling folks stuff they don't even want. As a matter of fact, you're so persuasive that you're able to sell people stuff that you know, and they know, is killing them."

Then I said, "That's a real talent. Imagine what God could do with somebody like you!" He was both floored and confused because no one had ever suggested to him that God could use him or that there was any place in God's Kingdom for his kind of skill. While I cannot condone the activity, the truth is, he did what was left him to do and he developed great skill in the midst of it.

There are a number of people just like this young man whom God has prepared on the streets and in the world that He is bringing into His Kingdom in this hour. They understand the world and its systems and aren't afraid to get right in the middle of it. And God is turning them around, changing their nature, and equipping them as seeds of deliverance to the very communities that prepared and raised them. Rarely does God use "church boys" to shake nations; more often He uses those who have been educated by the world, who know the language, the culture, the rules, and the players. They are people who are not intimidated by darkness because they've been delivered from the very heart of it. They're not fazed by clubs, crack houses, prisons, or those who call those places home. They're not intimidated by boardroom deals or the stress of Wall Street. Whatever the case, these are the very ones the enemy wants to snuff out before they can "amount to anything," because these seeds are dangerous. These seeds often produce great harvests.

Moses was the seed of deliverance for his day. Pharaoh determined that he was going to kill all of the male children of Israel because he had correctly deduced that God was about to raise up Moses as a deliverer for the entire nation. Meanwhile, God spoke to Moses' mother and had her prepare a basket for baby Moses, and she sent him floating downriver. In other words, he who was going to be the seed of deliverance became a *"basket case"* before he became a deliverer.

Moses was educated in Egypt, in a secular surrounding, because God knew that he was going to need to know more than "Kum-ba-yah" to reach his generation. There are actually some great benefits to growing up in Egypt. At the time of Moses and the Pharaohs, Egypt was one of the most advanced and civilized nations on the face of the earth. It was a renowned center for learning, boasting exceptional expertise in mathematics, physics, astronomy, and architecture. In addition, Egypt was home to the greatest historical library of the day.

There are biblical commentators, theologians, and historians who attribute the scenario of the burning bush capturing Moses' attention to his training in the Egyptian discipline of physics. How could a bush be engulfed in fire but not consumed? Moses saw the bush and, his curiosity aroused, said, "I will now turn aside and see this great sight, why the bush does not burn" (Ex. 3:3 NKJV). If the theologians are right, it was Moses' training in Egypt that drew his attention to the divine and ultimately to his call and responsibility. Egypt, then, was more than a great hiding place; it was also a center of opportunity to gain knowledge, insight, and perspective that could not necessarily be gained in the confined world or controlled environment of religious culture.

Perhaps you look like a basket case to those around you, but God sees you as a potential deliverer. It may appear to outsiders that you're going through hell, but God is raising you up to anoint you with the Holy Spirit.

God has been hiding a generation out in baskets so that the Church cannot ruin them. We're looking at a generation of people who seem to have drugged up and dropped out, and we have determined them to be "basket cases." But I submit to you that it is very possible that God has been hiding out this generation in order to protect them and to prepare them for His objectives and purposes. We must be careful not to judge previous conditions as either qualification or disqualification for God's use. He has been hiding out kids in world systems knowing that He can do more in one minute than what we can do in a thousand minutes or with a thousand messages. He can change their nature in an instant.

Recently God said something that blew my mind: "I sent Moses and Jesus into Egypt to protect them until the time of their revelation was at hand because there were those who wanted to kill them. Today the same is true—there are people I have been hiding in the world because those who seek to kill them are still alive in My Church. If I brought them in, 'church folk' would kill them by telling them, 'Your hair's too long, your hair's too short, take those earrings out of your nose,' and so on. I've been hiding them in the world until there is a church that is ready to receive them, until there is a group of people who will let them come as they are and dare to believe that the same God who kept, saved, and changed them is more than able to keep, save, and change today's generation as well."

The Spirit of God has given us a mandate to open the "X Files" and let a generation know that God has a way of taking broken, confused, lost "basket cases" and anointing them with the Holy Ghost, then turning them around and using them to infiltrate a generation. This generation of young people must understand that they are chosen, a royal priesthood, a holy nation, and a select people of God, uniquely gifted and anointed. There is a unique blessing upon them that has been upon no other generation on this planet.

There are two fundamental principles of God's modus operandi that I believe are especially relevant to this present generation. First, the Scripture clearly states, "Where sin abounded, grace abounded much more" (Rom. 5:20 NKJV). If that is true, and we know it is, we should expect that hovering just above the darkness, despair, attacks, and conspiracies that have been released upon our generation is a powerful anointing of God's enabling power. This power is able not only to penetrate this darkness, but also to shine a powerful light of glory. Therefore we must hold onto this promise, and by God's grace, rise to the occasion.

Second, the Scripture declares:

God has chosen the foolish things of the world to put to shame the wise, and God has chosen the weak things of the world to put to shame the things which are mighty; and the base things of the world and the things which are despised God has chosen, and the things which are not, to bring to nothing the things that are.

(1 Cor. 1:27–28 NKJV)

Isn't it just like God to raise up out of perhaps the most maligned and underestimated generation the modern age has ever seen, His greatest end-time champions? I think so! Therefore, we cry aloud without hesitation, "Let the sons of Egypt come forth." It is our time!

7

"your two sons, born to you in egypt, shall be mine"

We have established that God has a strategy of hiding His deliverers in Egypt, or among nonreligious people, until it is time for them to be revealed. We saw that He did this with Moses and Jesus; now we will see that God also employed this strategy with Ephraim and Manasseh. When the spirit of the age aims to kill the seed of deliverance, God will employ unorthodox methods to preserve His seed until its appointed time.

Jacob said:

And now your two sons, Ephraim and Manasseh, who were born to you in the land of Egypt before I came to you in Egypt, are mine; as Reuben and Simeon, they shall be mine. Your offspring whom you

beget after them shall be yours; they will be called by
the name of their brothers in their inheritance.

(Gen. 48:5–6 NKJV)

Jacob articulated to his son Joseph that he was
going to embrace Joseph's two boys, Ephraim and
Manasseh, the offspring of dream and vision. The boys
were born in Egypt, a type of the world, outside of
Israel, a type of the Church. In other words, they were
sired outside the realm of the covenant and perhaps
were even unaware that they had any relationship with
the covenant-bearing father. In this one act, Jacob
adopted them and placed them on equal status with his
two eldest sons, Reuben and Simeon. Jacob determined
to take these two pagan Egyptian boys and make them
his own flesh and blood, just as if they had been born
and raised within his home and the context of the
covenant.

As I read this portion of Scripture, the Spirit of God
began to speak to me and said, "Son, let Me show you
what I am prepared to do. I am bringing sons and
daughters who were born outside of covenant with Me,
and I am making them My own. I'm taking sons and
daughters born and raised in the secular environment,
who often know nothing about Me or My Church, and
I'm adopting them as My own children. They will not

be secondhand or second-class Christians; they will have access to all the blessing, privilege, and possession that those who have been raised in the church environment now have. I am looking for a generation of people who are not 'churchy' but who will understand that there is a covenant-keeping God in heaven and those who walk by His covenant will be blessed."

Look at what happened next in our narrative: "Then Israel saw Joseph's sons, and said, 'Who are these?' And Joseph said to his father, 'These are my sons, whom God has given me in this place'" (Gen. 48:8–9 NKJV).

This is amazing! Jacob spoke prophetically and possessively over sons who have not yet been clearly identified. He was talking about them, but he did not recognize who they were as Joseph presented them to him. Jacob was saying in essence, "Those boys of yours who were born in Egypt—I'm going to bless them, they're going to be mine, I'm going to anoint them, and they're going to be called by my name." But when Ephraim and Manasseh actually stood in front of him, Israel didn't recognize them and asked, "Who are these?"

Joseph responded by telling him, "Dad, these are the kids you were just talking about—you know, the ones you just said you're going to bless, anoint, and use . . ."

Isn't that interesting? Is it possible to speak prophetically over a generation and then not recognize them when you see them? Of course, it is possible, and it is happening here for at least a couple of reasons. First of all, the text tells us that Israel's eyes were dim—he had in some degree lost vision and the ability to see clearly. This could have been one reason why Israel did not recognize the boys when they came. To draw a parallel with today, a Church who is dim in vision—who has allowed itself to become obsolete and antiquated in regard to vision and illumination—will not be able to recognize the very instruments God has provided to renew and revive them.

Second, it is possible to speak prophetically over a generation and not recognize them when we see them because they do not appear as we expected. Ephraim and Manasseh were probably not dressed in traditional Hebrew clothing because they were born and raised in Egypt. Most likely they were dressed like Egyptians, perhaps wearing replicas of bronze cobras wrapped around their heads, bracelets on their arms, along with lots of gold and bright colors that were no doubt shocking to the traditional Hebrew mind. So the question, "Who are these?" arose in part perhaps because they did not look as Israel expected them to look.

Does that sound at all familiar? Today's generation

does not come wearing floor-length dresses or three-piece suits. They come wearing FUBU and Hilfiger, Calvin Klein and Prada. They come wearing what they've carefully selected from swap meets and resale shops. They come wearing their own kinds of cobras and hardware, with rings through their noses and tattoos on their arms. Consequently, much of the Church is saying, "Who are these?" Understand that many of them don't even know who they are yet, but what they look like does not disqualify them from divine usefulness.

God, the covenant-bearing Father, has been speaking prophetic words and declaring promises of destiny over their lives, and they don't yet realize that they belong to Him. He has been calling them by name and extending His hands to cover, bless, and anoint them; He wants to give them His name as their own. As a matter of fact, many of them, without realizing it, have been under the providential hand of God's care throughout their lives.

Some of you reading this book, as you reflect, can recognize the hand of God covering and guiding your life, even in seasons when you thought you were far from Him. I submit to you that God has actually made an investment in this generation—that He has covered and protected you—and in the coming days He will be looking for a return on that investment.

I believe that Israel's questioning response is typical of much of the modern-day Church's response. We look at this generation born and raised in Egypt and wonder, "Can God use them?" "Who are these?" It's not a matter of "Can God save them?" because He has purposed to save them from the beginning. It's not a matter of "Can God use them?" for that's been the plan from the beginning of time. As revolutionary as it may seem, God is reaching His powerful arm of destiny outside of the nominal Church to arrest sons and daughters who have been born and raised separated from Him and His covenant. He is beginning to bring them into the Kingdom for His glory. These are the offspring of Joseph, the sons of dream, vision, and strength, and they belong to the Church and to the Kingdom of God. The dreams and the visions that are in them, even though they have been raised in Egypt, are God's, and He is determined to be glorified through them.

An amazing reversal is about to transpire. Those of us who consider ourselves learned men and women of Scripture, doctors of religion, Bible teachers and students, are going to watch in amazement and in some cases bewilderment as sons and daughters from Egypt, recently saved from crack houses and Wall Street boardrooms, lift their voices to declare the Word of God to their generation. Churches of thousands will spring up under the leadership of children born in Egypt who have heard the call of the covenant-bearing Father and come to Him to be blessed. Perhaps they will not know our Greek and Hebrew, but they will be speaking a language that their generation understands. That's what time it is.

The covenant-bearing Father is circumventing the arrogance of our religiosity and anointing a generation with His glory, who we are certain are unqualified— their caps are on backwards, their jeans are dragging, and they're wearing tennis shoes in church.

Be prepared! Sons and daughters born in Egypt are on their way, and they're headed for a church near you with earrings through their noses, lips, and eyebrows. Will you recognize them when they get there?

One final thought before we move on. I submit to you that this generation who are on their way has not rejected Christianity; they have rejected "Churchanity." I am not saying that they haven't been to church; I am suggesting that too often what they received when they got there was not Christ. Instead, they got our rules, our regulations, and in many cases our judgmentalism. The sad fact is that it is possible to go to church for several years in this nation and never meet Christ. I am convinced that what Jesus said to the woman at the well is still true: "If you knew the gift of God, and who it is who says to you, 'Give Me a drink,' you would have asked Him, and He would have given you living water" (John 4:10 NKJV). When people come to know the gift of God, they will ask us for Him; we will not have to ask them.

In regard to this generation that has rejected not our Christ, but our religion, let us consider the powerful thing Jesus said as He rebuked the Pharisees.

> But woe to you, scribes and Pharisees, hypocrites! For you shut up the kingdom of heaven against men; for you neither go in yourselves, nor do you allow those who are entering to go in . . . Woe to you, scribes and Pharisees, hypocrites! For you travel land and sea to win one proselyte [or, You conduct crusades and revivals and preach on TV to win a convert], and when he is won, you make him twice as much a son of hell as yourselves.
>
> (Matt. 23:13, 15 NKJV)

Jesus was saying to them, "You will not enter into the Kingdom of God (not the Church), and you hinder those who desire to come in because of your religion and tradition." I submit that in some degree, God has done many of our young people a favor by keeping them out of church until now because they will not have to unlearn our tradition in order to manifest God's Kingdom. I know this sounds strange, but remember, God is not the God of just the Church—He is the God of the whole earth. Jehosaphat said, "O LORD God of our fathers, are You not God in heaven, and do You not rule over all the kingdoms of the nations, and in Your hand is there not power and might, so that no one is able to withstand You?" (2 Chron. 20:6 NKJV) The answer to all those questions, of course, is yes. Therefore, is it not possible that God could put His dreams and His vision in people that He knows belong to Him but do not yet belong to us?

I say with resolute certainty that there is a generation upon the face of the earth that God has placed His dream and vision within. They are pregnant with possibility, but because they are coming out of Egypt, much of the Church has written them off. Hear the voice of the Spirit of God, "Your two sons, Ephraim and Manasseh, who were born to you in the land of Egypt before I came to you in Egypt, are mine; as Reuben and Simeon, they shall be mine" (Gen. 48:5 NKJV).

8

behold, the
dreamer cometh

In considering what to do with the message God had given me, my attention returned to Jacob, Joseph, Ephraim, and Manasseh. Somehow I knew that I had to go back in order to accurately look ahead. What were the thoughts that captivated Joseph as he prepared his sons for an encounter with blessing at the hands of their grandfather? Was he remembering his own upbringing and exodus in Egypt? What had transpired that allowed him to stand at this juncture with his own sons, awaiting the transfer of blessing from the covenant-carrying father to the next generation?

Joseph's father, the patriarch Jacob, had produced twelve sons. Jacob's favorite offspring was his eleventh son, Joseph; he was the dreamer. Hated by his brothers because of their father's favor and because of his dreams, Joseph further alienated himself from his siblings by telling them about a dream in which they bowed before him. "There we were, binding sheaves in the field. Then behold, my sheaf arose and also stood upright; and indeed your sheaves stood all around and bowed down to my sheaf" (Gen. 37:7 NKJV).

A dream can be a very powerful thing, sometimes dividing people before it unites them. For some reason, people with dreams and vision are often ostracized, even hated, by others. I have always found this to be curious, because any dreamer will tell you that no one is responsible for what he or she dreams. This is especially true when it comes to the dreams and visions that the Holy Spirit places within a person. They are given from above, and we are only the recipients of them, not the originators.

Whenever God begins to do something powerful through an individual, He usually initiates it with a dream or a vision because dreams and visions are the language of the Holy Spirit. God said that in the last days, "I will pour out My Spirit on all flesh / . . . Your old men shall dream dreams, / Your young men shall see visions" (Joel 2:28 NKJV). Whenever God begins to do something in the heart of a man, he usually begins it with a dream.

Perhaps you have already recognized that the

enemy hates dreams and dreamers. As we come to understand the power and potential of dreams and visions inspired by the Holy Spirit, we will more clearly understand this deep aversion. You see, a dream or a vision of the Spirit is not something that *will be*, but something that already *is established* in the realm of the heavenlies. God reveals no works in progress, only completed works. Dreams therefore take us beyond what is and show us what is to be.

The narrative continues:

> Now Israel loved Joseph more than all his children, because he was the son of his old age. Also he made him a tunic of many colors. But when his brothers saw that their father loved him more than all his brothers, they hated him and could not speak peaceably to him.
>
> (Gen. 37:3–4 NKJV)

Jacob gave his favorite son a special gift, a "coat of many colors," which was an embroidered full-length jacket or tunic. Created with extraordinary craftsmanship, the coat contained every color imaginable.

More than just a jacket, this garment was representative of God Himself. The Bible declares that "God is light and in Him is no darkness at all" (1 John 1:5

NKJV). One day as I was meditating about the significance of Joseph's coat, the Spirit of the Lord said to me, "Son, consider light."

"Light?" I replied. "What does light have to do with the coat?"

"Light contains every color within it. Every color of the spectrum is embodied within light. Son, this coat is representative of Me and light, illumination, and revelation. The multicolored coat is a type of the illumination and revelation of the Holy Spirit."

As we further consider this story, it is essential that we recognize the broad use of type and shadow in this narrative. Clothed with revelation and understanding, Joseph's purpose was to bring redemption, illumination, and salvation to the entire world of his time. He had the light of the covenant Father upon him. The coat of many colors was representative of the gift of God's light and vision to Joseph. It is significant to consider that the coat was given to Joseph by his father Jacob, who was the patriarchal father, the carrier of covenant and promise.

Whenever Joseph wore the jacket, it reminded his brothers of what they were not. They were not favored by their father. They did not have a coat of many colors. They did not have illumination, understanding, dreams, or vision. To Joseph, however, the coat was a reminder that he was chosen and favored, endowed with special gifts and abilities. Joseph is representative of a generation who has God's favor. He was chosen. While many people are called by God, few are chosen by Him. It takes more than a call to do the work of God—it also takes dream, vision, and illumination.

Dreams and vision, light and illumination are critical in order that we might know the mind of God and His ways. They dispel darkness and allow us to see where we are and where we are going. Vision is one of the most critical aspects of ministry; without it, we are doomed to tradition and mediocrity. I believe that God desires to pour greater anointing, greater power, and greater revelation into our generation so that we are not just reading about revivals of old, but are experiencing great revival in our day. When we search history and read Scripture, we find that great moves of God, great churches, and great visitations of the Spirit were not simply products of people who followed tradition; instead, they got a revelation from God for themselves and began to do the will of God.

Perhaps you are familiar with the rest of Joseph's story. Jacob sent Joseph to check up on his brothers, who were out tending sheep. When his brothers saw him coming, they plotted to kill him. (Notice that those without dream or vision are almost always at odds with those who dream, because dreamers expose those who are without vision both for what they are and for what they are not.) Fed up, Joseph's brothers kidnapped him and stripped him of his coat of many colors. Despite his frantic pleas, Joseph's brothers threw him into a pit to die and tore up his coat of many colors.

Perhaps they thought they were destroying Joseph's illumination, dream, and vision. In actuality they'd only removed that which was representative of light and illumination; dream and vision were still very much alive inside him.

Vision and revelation are not in what we wear or what we do. They are not in mimicking those who exhibit expertise or understanding of these arenas. Dream and vision reside on the inside. Joseph's brothers could not confiscate the gifts, only the representation of them.

Jacob's fourth son, Judah, came up with a "brilliant" idea. "What profit is there if we kill our brother and conceal his blood? Come and let us sell him" (Gen. 37:26–27 NKJV). So those who had put Joseph into a pit pulled him back out and sold him to traveling merchants bound for Egypt. Joseph's brothers had to quickly cover up what they had done, so they dipped Joseph's coat in a goat's blood and returned to their father, who believed a wild beast had devoured the favored son.

Once in Egypt, the merchants sold Joseph into the service of the captain of Pharaoh's guard. There, with God's help, he prospered and soon was placed in charge of Potiphar's entire household. Even while working as a servant, the favored son continued to find favor. The Bible records that Potiphar's household was actually blessed because of Joseph's presence.

Unfortunately, Joseph's good looks attracted the unwanted attention of his master's wife, who attempted to seduce him. When Joseph refused her, she falsely accused him of rape, and he was imprisoned. Despite this betrayal, Joseph's gifts and talent were soon recognized by the prison warden, who put him in charge of all prisoners. The son of Jacob's favor continued to experience the Lord's favor as well.

During his imprisonment Joseph correctly interpreted dreams for the temporarily imprisoned royal butler and baker. He asked that the butler remember him to Pharaoh upon his release. The butler forgot, so Joseph remained in prison for another two years until Pharaoh himself had dreams that needed interpretation. He summoned Joseph, and God enabled the son of favor to explain Pharaoh's dreams of forthcoming abundance and famine in Egypt. Pharaoh recognized the hand of the Lord upon Joseph and put him in charge of the resources for the entire nation. At age thirty, Joseph was responsible for collecting and storing the harvest for all of Egypt during its years of abundance. During this period Pharaoh gave Joseph a wife, and two sons were born: Manasseh and Ephraim.

Then the predicted famine ravaged the region, and Joseph's strategic planning saved Egypt from starvation. Along with tens of thousands of desperate pilgrims traveling from Canaan, Joseph's brothers arrived in Egypt in search of food. When they appeared at the royal court, Joseph immediately recognized them. The dream that Joseph had nearly two decades earlier was fulfilled as his brothers bowed before him. As governor, Joseph put his brothers through several tests until he could restrain himself no longer. When he finally revealed his true identity, he tried to comfort his stunned brothers by saying, "Do not therefore be grieved or angry with yourselves because you sold me here; for God sent me before you to preserve life" (Gen. 45:5 NKJV).

To further understand the significance of Joseph's story today, we must recognize that Joseph is a type and shadow, or a representation of the end-time Church. He was the favored son of a covenant-bearing father who was chosen to carry the anointing of covenant to his generation. He was the favored son, filled with dreams and vision, who was sent to save the world. How apropos this model is for today. We live in a world that is spiritually famished. The only entity suited to provide the relief that is necessary is the Church. By the power of the Holy Spirit, through the illumination of dreams and vision, we are given the direction and answers for a world that often doesn't even know the right questions to ask. A Church void of dreamers and visionaries, however, cannot supply answers to a visionless and drifting world. It is of supreme importance in this hour that the Church, like Joseph, be fully clothed in the mantle of revelation, illumination, dream, and vision.

Joseph's dream was of siblings bowing before him, but it was more important and far reaching than that; it was a picture of what a dream does. A dream or a vision automatically elevates the dreamer. A dream gives dominion because it triggers an ability to see things that other people do not. The Church is supposed to be seeing what this world has lost its ability to perceive. We are supposed to have insight, favor, and understanding beyond that of our fellow man.

To recap, Joseph went from the pit to the palace to prison and finally to power. I have discovered that every step up in the Kingdom of God is first preceded by one step down in the flesh. Joseph went down into the pit and then up into the palace. He went down into the prison and then up into power. There are ups and downs—or rather, downs and ups—in serving God within Kingdom living. It helps to understand that God takes us down and then up so that every time we go down, we can be assured that the situation is temporary and that the next step is up!

For years Jacob thought his son Joseph, the son of favor, was dead. Remember, Joseph symbolizes the end-time Church. There is a remnant church today that has been thought dead and that has been told it is powerless, dreamless, and without vision whom God is raising from obscurity and has marked to deliver nations. Many today think the Church is impotent and irrelevant, but I declare to you, as we move forward in this twenty-first century, God is putting His Church back on Main Street. The sons and daughters of dream and vision are going to take center stage at the culmination of the ages.

Jacob sent his sons to Egypt in search of food in order to preserve his family. When they arrived, Joseph immediately recognized that they were the brothers who sold him into captivity. Herein lies another revelation. The generation of people whom God is about to use have been rejected, maligned, placed in pits, and left to die. They have been told that they will never amount to anything. Yet, they are the very ones whom God is raising up to preserve the nation in this last day.

When everything is "going to hell in a handbasket," it is the children of light, clothed in the illumination of the Holy Ghost, who are to bring answers and divine solutions. In the narrative, it was Joseph, the abused and rejected brother, who had the ability and responsibility to restore a nation gripped by famine. Joseph's brothers never imagined that he would one day provide for them. The same is true today. The world seems to be no longer looking for their brother, the Church, whom they know exists but perceive as irrelevant and impotent to provide answers or assistance. But the truth is, the Church, like Joseph, has not only survived and endured, but is now, through its dreams and vision, prepared to occupy the seat of authority. In the coming days, the Church, like Joseph, will more visibly provide the world with interpretations of dreams that they cannot interpret themselves and will instruct the world on how to make it through seasons of famine and need.

When Joseph revealed himself to his brothers, he declared, "You meant this for evil, but God turned it around for good. You tried to kill me, but all the time you were trying to destroy me, God had a vision and a dream in me to preserve you."

Beloved, God is going to use the dream and the vision that reside within you to bring life to some of the very ones who have been trying to discredit you. You are the one that God is going to use. He has put the dream and vision, gifts and ability within you, and He will position His children of dream and vision to assume places and positions of notoriety and influence.

Joseph was taken captive to Egypt initially against his will, but God used Egypt as a training ground for him. Some of you reading these words right now are in captivity. You've seemingly been left in a pit and abandoned in prison, but the reality is that, like Joseph, you have been fruitful wherever you are. Your fruit is going to bless the nations in the last days.

9

who are these?

then Israel saw Joseph's sons, and said, 'Who are these?'" (Gen. 48:8 NKJV). Jacob's ability to speak prophetically, yet his inability to recognize whom he was speaking about, is not just an important point, but a powerful element for the receiving and releasing of what we have come to call the X Blessing. It also provides the context for the discussion and development of the power that will be ours when the Church uses its God-given ability to spiritually discern.

Understand that the X Blessing will not be received or released by a carnally minded church with a non-spiritual perspective. In order to receive and walk in this blessing, we must exercise a spiritual maturity that, unfortunately, is all too unique in our modern religious systems. *The X Blessing is, in essence, the drawing near of unidentified sons so that they may be identified by covenant people; it is the adoption by the covenant-bearing Father of sons that are born in Egypt.* This means that the Father's representatives must be able to recognize and identify these sons born in Egypt, even when they do not know who they are. To do this, we must take on a perspective that is much more Christlike and much less "religious."

God is omniscient, which simply means there is nothing beyond the scope of His knowing. We, on the other hand, the apostle Paul says, "see through a glass, darkly . . . We know in part, and we prophesy in part" (1 Cor. 13:12, 9 KJV). Yet God has given us His Spirit, the Scripture says, "that we might know the things that have been freely given to us by God" (1 Cor. 2:12 NKJV). That includes the harvest and the seeds of deliverance that are resident within a generation. The Spirit of God has been given to us, in part, that we might be able to know and recognize these sons and daughters of God, born in Egypt, even when they don't know who they are. Now, obviously, this task is not for the faint of heart because it entails stepping beyond and outside of the realms and regions of that which is comfortable, usual, or ordinary. The religious mind would not have gone to Zaccheus's house; the religious mind would never have allowed Mary to pour an alabaster box of ointment at the feet of the Messiah; the religious mind would not have allowed a Syro-Phoenecian woman to receive healing for her daughter or would never have allowed Peter to preach in Cornelius's house.

Once my mind began to open to this truth, the Spirit of God began to deal with me and said, "Son, you are passing by sons and daughters of Mine all the time, and you don't even recognize who they are. You're interacting with them on airplanes, and you see them on television and in movies, you hear their music, and you do not even recognize that they belong to Me. I am going to begin to show you My Egyptian sons and daughters. I'm going to begin to identify them to you."

How often do we sit across from someone at lunch whom God has desired to use for His glory, but for some reason we have already written him or her off as outside of the realm of God's usability? Let me challenge you by saying that God is going to place people in front of you whom He desires you talk to. He wants to use you and me to identify sons and daughters raised in Egypt who are marked for Kingdom purpose.

Some time ago, as I was looking at the significant percentage of young men in the Church who are raised in only matriarchal homes, the Lord placed within my heart the desire to bless them. This desire was birthed as I read the account recorded in Luke 2, where Mary and Joseph found Jesus, then a twelve-year-old boy, in the Temple with the religious leaders of the day. The significance of that event occurring when Jesus was just twelve hit me, and the Lord put on my heart that we needed to start giving our young men a sense of purpose. I was seven years old when I first began to recognize the call of God upon my life; when I was nearly twelve, I was sure of it. Thankfully, I was raised in a godly home where parents taught me the responsibility of knowing and having a relationship with God.

Every Father's Day at Church of the Harvest, we dedicate our evening gathering to consecrating our twelve-year-old boys to the Lord. During the service, each young man receives his own Bible and we challenge him to develop disciplines in reading the Word of God, in practicing prayer, and in pursuing righteousness. In addition, each young man receives a medallion that looks much like an Olympic medal. We want our young men to know that before they even get started, they're already winners because they are in relationship with Jesus Christ. The young men also receive an inscribed silver dog tag on a chain that symbolizes the fact that they are now warriors in God's army.

I've already discussed the fact that this present generation lacks many of the foundational and fundamental elements that enable a society to progress. Twenty-five or thirty years ago, we could assume that the fourteen-year-old boy we heard cursing on the street corner, or the fifteen-year-old youth with a gun, or the thirteen-year-old girl who is sexually active, had learned in his or her home some measure of right and wrong. Each understood the parameters of what was and wasn't acceptable, and he or she knowingly chose one or the other. We can no longer take that type of training for granted.

Again, this is why I say this generation is not rebellious; they are ignorant. If the Church is to model the fullness of Christ and the Kingdom of God, we must do more than just save souls; we must also redeem culture. This means supplying a generation with those things that are lacking in areas beyond fundamental spirituality, including social graces, etiquette, teaching young men to be gentlemen, and teaching young women to be ladies.

The special consecration service I mentioned is not just for our young men. We also present our young women before the Lord with equal reverence and expectation. Many of our young women participate in a twelve-month program called the Esther Project.® This project includes biblical instruction about Bible study, prayer, spiritual gifts, relationships, marriage, and parenting, as well as training for business and careers. We take the apostle Paul's exhortation to Titus as a model:

> The older men should be sober, reverent, temperate, sound in faith, in love, in patience; the older women likewise, that they be reverent in behavior, not slanderers, not given to much wine, teachers of good things—that they admonish the young women to love their husbands, to love their children, to be discreet, chaste, homemakers, good, obedient to their own husbands, that the word of God may not be blasphemed.
>
> (Titus 2:2–5 NKJV)

Some would say that contextually, in the Hebrew culture and biblical times, this would be appropriate, but of course, today in our modern culture, we must teach our young women to do more things. For example, this list doesn't say anything about their being doctors or lawyers or preachers or whatever they want to be. We must understand the context. The apostle Paul is addressing the role that the *Church should play* in instructing women; he is not saying that women are limited to doing these things but saying that these areas are our responsibility to teach them. A woman can be a doctor, a lawyer, a preacher, or anything else. But the

Church's responsibility is to teach the skills and disciplines listed in Titus 2 because, while it was perhaps expected within the culture of that day, it cannot be assumed within the culture of our day.

Because we understand that our young people are destined to lead their generation and eventually a nation, we do not leave it to school systems or boys and girls clubs to prepare our young people for their future. We purposefully invest in them and pray for them, believing that "no weapon formed against [them] shall prosper" (Isa. 54:17 NKJV) and contending that everything they are purposed for will be fulfilled.

After our most recent consecration service, two young men stopped to talk with me. I was so moved as one of the boys looked me in the eye and said, "Bishop, this has been the best day of my life. Thank you." The young man standing next to him added, "Bishop, my goal is to play in the NBA and to be even better than Kobe Bryant." He was dead serious as he continued, "By the way, I'm going to dedicate my first championship ring to you." I love that kind of vision!

10

seeing what simeon saw

the X Blessing is the drawing near of unidentified sons to the covenant father for the purpose of receiving his blessing. The same need exists today for the yet unrecognized sons and daughters of God. They must be identified and brought to the Father for the release of His blessing upon their lives.

In Genesis 48, when Joseph presented Ephraim and Manasseh before their grandfather, Jacob asked, "Who are these?" and Joseph responded, "These are my sons whom God has given me in this place." And Israel replied, "Please bring them to me, and I will bless them." In other words, Israel was saying that these unknown sons must be drawn near to him.

As I further considered this truth, the Spirit of God led me to the gospel of Luke and illuminated the story of Simeon. "And behold, there was a man in Jerusalem whose name was Simeon, and this man was just and devout, waiting for the Consolation of Israel, and the Holy Spirit was upon him" (Luke 2:25 NKJV). *Consolation* means "the drawing near," so this verse actually reads that Simeon was waiting for the nation of Israel to once again be drawn near to God or for Israel (the Church) to come back into its destiny and purpose. Simeon knew that there was an anointing that would bring comfort and deliverance to the house of God and reestablish the people of God back into their rightful place and relationship.

Simeon's posture and expectation are nothing short of amazing. No prophet had spoken on behalf of God since Malachi. While religious ritual continued in the form of sacrifices, festivals, and worship in the temple, God had not spoken prophetically to His people for more than four centuries. In spite of this silence, Simeon was expectantly waiting for God to draw His people near Him again.

The Bible records that Simeon was a devout man. He knew that something was coming that would be greater than what had ever been seen or experienced before, and he was expectantly waiting for God to do what He had promised. I understand that kind of expectation. Like Simeon, I am waiting and looking for something I have not yet seen with my natural eyes but that I have tasted in my spirit. I sincerely believe that my generation is going to experience a revival and a renewal the likes of which have not been seen before on earth. John Wesley did not see what we are going to see. Neither did Charles Finney, Charles Spurgeon, or Aimee Semple McPherson.

The Bible declares that in the last days, "I will pour out My Spirit on all flesh" (Joel 2:28 NKJV). What an extraordinary promise that is. Perhaps some of you reading this book right now are waiting for God to visit sons and daughters and to pour out His Spirit upon them. You may be waiting for your kids to get off crack or your relatives to get out of prison. You're praying for your parents, uncles, aunts, nephews, and nieces to receive a revelation of God, because they are trapped in false religions and witchcraft, they're deceived by paganism and occultism, and you're waiting for something to break the back of the devil. I'm telling you it's on the way. It is coming through a visitation of the Spirit of God and it's coming through the hearts, minds, hands, and feet of people who are not religious but who are spiritual.

The story of Simeon continues, "The Holy Spirit was upon him" (Luke 2:25 NKJV). What we as believers need now more than a church membership card is the Holy Spirit upon us. More than a personalized pew with our brass signature plaque, more than a position in some ministry, we need the power and the anointing of the Holy Spirit; only He can enable us to move and flow in this anointing. He is the only One who can navigate us through what eyes cannot see and what ears cannot hear. He is the only One able to reveal what other people aren't hearing.

Perhaps you're wondering if it's really possible for religious ritual to go on for years and for God to have said nothing. Yes, and I contend that it's even possible to have large churches and huge ministries and yet to lack a prophetic unction from God that tells you what time it is or what you're supposed to do. I believe that it is absolutely possible for religion to operate and for God to be nowhere in the midst of it.

The Word says, "This man was just and devout, waiting for the Consolation of Israel, and the Holy Spirit was upon him. And it had been revealed . . . " (Luke 2:25–26 NKJV). There had been a divine unveiling—the Spirit of God disclosed something that was hidden to the natural eye. Other covenant people were not seeing it, but Simeon was expectantly waiting for God. The Bible reveals that one day while he was waiting, the Holy Spirit pulled back the cover and showed him that he would not see death until he had seen the Lord's Christ. The Spirit said, "Simeon, you will not die until you see this revival; you're not leaving here until you see a move of God. You are going to witness with your own eyes the manifestation that prophets and preachers have spoken of for hundreds of years."

The same is possible today for those who will see with eyes of the Spirit and who will not be led by emotion or by intellect, but by the proceeding Word of God. Like Simeon, we are called to see a move of God and we are destined to watch for the anointing. It is interesting to consider that Simeon was neither a prophet nor a priest—he was not one of the men to whom God would have traditionally revealed Himself. As we have seen, however, God often alters His rules and goes around His ordinances and chooses the unexpected to reveal Himself to. Simeon was simply a Holy Spirit-anointed man.

"And when the parents brought in the Child Jesus, to do for Him according to the custom of the law, [Simeon] took Him up in his arms and blessed God" (Luke 2:27–28 NKJV). Get this! The religious world was carrying on business as usual, and Simeon was on his way to the Temple. He had no idea why; all he knew was that the Holy Spirit was leading him. (Rest assured that deliverers and people who are spiritual are always doing things that religious people think they ought not to do.) On the same day, Mary took baby Jesus to the

Temple, according to the custom of the Law, to be circumcised by the priest. As Mary was preparing to hand Jesus to the priest, Simeon intercepted Jesus before He was put into the priest's hands. In other words, Simeon intercepted Jesus before He was put into the hands of organized religion. Simeon recognized by the Spirit of God that this was a child of destiny.

In these last days, if we are going to recognize those who have been raised in the world, whom God has marked, we are going to have to be spiritual. God is going to identify those who are marked for Kingdom purpose to His prophetic people. *Interception*—that's what the Church is about to do with sons and daughters raised in Egypt. Today God is calling sons and daughters that organized religion cannot handle. He needs people who will be led by the Spirit: people who will dare to go where others won't go, who will say what others won't say, and who can see what others can't see. It's time for us to intercept designs of the enemy—plans to destroy, to kill, to steal, and to rob a generation of revival. We must intercept those who are marked for the Kingdom.

God is looking for "spiritual Simeons" who will intercept seeds of deliverance before they are put into the hands of organized religion and castrated instead of circumcised. Religion castrates; it robs a person of his or her ability to reproduce. We have too many castrated sons and too many mutilated daughters. We take warriors and champions, gifts of God, and we bring them into the Church and we castrate them: "You can't do this, you can't do that. We don't do it like that, we do it like this."

Have you ever considered the difference between circumcision and castration? It's simply where you cut. Cut too much, and you leave children with no ability to reproduce. If we are careless, ignorant, or cruel, we take their gifts, their anointing, and their calling and we render them null and void. God is anointing a people to intercept a whole generation before they come into the hands of religion and get castrated. We have to sanctify, but not sterilize, them.

Let's return to our primary text of Genesis 48. Jacob said of Manasseh and Ephraim, "Bring them here so that I can bless them." Jacob was saying in essence, "These boys were born in Egypt, but I recognize now who they are, so bring them to me so that I can bless them. Although they are gifted, intelligent, and equipped, they still must be anointed."

Again, the X Blessing is the drawing near by the Spirit of God of unidentified sons so that covenant people may identify them and they may receive God's blessing. There are many people outside the Church who have gifts from God. Ephesians 4 instructs:

But to each one of us grace was given according to the measure of Christ's gift. Therefore He says:

"When He ascended on high,
He led captivity captive,
And gave gifts to men."

. . . And He Himself gave some to be apostles, some prophets, some evangelists, and some pastors and teachers.

(Eph. 4:7–8, 11 NKJV)

If we read carefully, we will observe that Christ did not give these gifts to the Church, He gave them to men and to women. Some of them are inside the Church and some are resident outside of the Church. Once gifts are given, men and women can use the gifts wherever they want. If they use them for God, the blessing of the Lord and His preservation will rest upon them. If they choose to use the gifts outside of God's will, they will bear the consequences for that choice. But the gifts are given to *people,* not to the institution of the Church.

Let me give an example. I have been endowed with a gift of persuasion that is essential to my evangelistic and prophetic responsibilities. Now, I could take this gift and use it to sell cars, insurance, real estate—you name it, and I could close just about any deal. Instead

of using my gifts to explain the gospel and the Kingdom of God, I could be one of the best con artists
you've ever seen. The fact is, the gifts will work any-
where. They are given to individuals, and each person
must choose, and eventually give an account for, how
he or she uses the gifts that God gave him or her.

Understand that there are several dimensions of
anointing. One dimension is the anointing that resides
within an individual and accompanies a gift. Another
dimension of anointing comes from above or beyond
the gifted. This is a protective anointing, a blessing
that guards and preserves the use of the gift for ministry and sanctifies it for service in the Kingdom of
God. No matter how gifted or anointed a person may
be, that gift is not maximized in glorifying God or edi-
fying His body until it is recognized and affirmed by
those who are in covenant with the God who gave the
gift. It is for this reason that we lay hands on people
and set them apart for works of ministry. We do not
gift them; rather, we affirm and bless them.

That is what Jacob did with Ephraim and Manasseh.
He recognized that although Joseph's boys were born in
Egypt, there was something of the destiny of God in
those boys' souls. Jacob said, "I don't care where they
were born or where they were equipped, they belong to
me." And God is saying of this generation, "I don't care

what side of the tracks you are on; I don't care who you've been working for; I don't care who schooled you. You belong to Me and I'm about to get what is Mine!"

They're coming from the north, south, east, and west. They're coming from the club and the disco, from the gangs and from the whorehouse, from the crack house and from the streets. They're coming from the universities, office complexes, marketplace, and Wall Street. They're coming as single parents, and they're coming married with kids. They're coming!

It is time for the veil to be pulled from our eyes. It is not only the world's eyes that have been blinded, but, in some cases, ours as well. The reason that some people have not come into the Kingdom of God yet is not because their eyes are blind, but because ours are. God says, "If you'll open your eyes, I am going to show you brothers and sisters of yours, sons and daughters of Mine, whom you have not identified yet. The religious will miss it—they may even be appalled by it. People shrouded in religion will not be able to walk this line because they are going to be looking for cookie cutouts of themselves. They're looking for folks who walk, talk, and sound just like themselves."

Peter was driving toward the marina when his pager went off. He didn't recognize the phone number, but he reached for his cell phone to return the call. A woman's voice answered: "Yes, baby, this is Gracie . . ."

Peter's mind raced, *Gracie? Baby? I don't think I know a Gracie.* Before he could answer, Gracie had spewed a trail of seduction, and he realized immediately that Gracie was a call girl trying to hook up with one of her "johns." Peter interrupted and let her know that she definitely had the wrong number, but, prompted by the Holy Spirit, he asked, "Do you go to church?"

That was not a question that Gracie was expecting. She ditched her seductive voice and became a regular woman. "Well, yeah, I used to go to church, but it became so much pressure, keepin' up with the right clothes and the right look just to be accepted. I couldn't do it anymore."

Peter assured her that wasn't church but religion and he was sorry that had been her experience. "Gracie, what you're looking for in your johns isn't real; it's fake, and it's potentially deadly. You need to return to what is authentic. Only God can truly satisfy you. Gracie—by the way, is that your real name?" he asked.

"No, my name is Kelly."

"Kelly, do you realize how much God loves you? It's no accident that your page came to me instead of your other appointment. God loves you and wants your attention."

"I'll just bet you my grandmother is praying for me right now. Somehow she always knows," Kelly said, laughing. "Peter, would it be OK if I called you again sometime, not for anything weird, but just because you're a nice man?"

"That would be fine, Kelly. Here's the number."

Two or three months passed before Peter heard from Kelly again. She had moved from Los Angeles back home to Houston, where she had been offered an excellent job with the phone company. She had found a vibrant and healthy church that she was excited to be a part of. Kelly told Peter that the catalyst for change had been her "accidental" phone call to him and how grateful she was to be in relationship with a God who never took His eyes off her.

Interception! That's what time it is.

11

next?

i was born a veritable church baby, the second son of a pastor who was a jurisdictional prelate in the denomination in which I was raised. Both he and my mother were active in local and national church responsibilities, and when I say that I was raised in church, I am not exaggerating. From the time I was born until I was sixteen or seventeen years old, I spent five to six days each week in church services, youth or junior choir rehearsals, youth or junior usher board meetings, the missionary fellowship that my mother taught, and the brotherhood fellowships that my father taught. I lived in church, and although it was not the most enjoyable place to be as a kid, in retrospect I am very thankful for my Christian upbringing.

I was raised around people who instilled in me a steadfast faith and love for God. As I began to grow, however, I also experienced the frustration of many young people who are raised in church. In my situation, I came to recognize that many of the people who were good churchgoing people were also very negative when adversity came upon them. They loved God with a steadfast, emotional love, but their love was somewhat scripturally uninformed. By that I mean they displayed the emotion, the affection, and the mental assent to loving God, but when it came to practical "doing the Word of God" when they were in trouble, they were challenged.

As I began to read Scripture, I did not find in Jesus or in those who followed Him this negativity. Jesus said, "If you love Me, keep My commandments" (John 14:15 NKJV). Jesus elevated love from mere emotion or a physical activity (including going to church) to a standard of hands-on obedience to Him at all times. Obviously, none of us is perfect, yet one of the things that became very important to me was that in all things I try to hit the mark.

It is interesting that as I began to read Scripture for myself, and not simply take the religion and the traditions handed to me, that I began to see in the Word a new side of God and His people. I began to see that God's people were not constantly sick, poor, or complaining. I began to recognize that poverty did not equate with holiness, and sickness was not God's methodology for teaching His people lessons. It was at this point that I began to inquire and even to question, not with a rebellious spirit but with a revolutionary one, many of the things that had been held as truth by the religious generation that preceded me. The more I learned the truth of the Scripture for myself, the more I recognized that there was a perspective that had to be altered if my generation was going to press beyond the accomplishments or righteousness of the generation that preceded ours.

I like to take biblical texts and stories and try to apply them to our modern context. Over the years these narratives have helped me understand various aspects of the Kingdom of God and how it is meant to work. Something I began to realize was that every time Moses spoke the Word of the Lord to the children of Israel, and every time the children of Israel, under Moses' leadership, witnessed one of God's miracles, they had literally been to church. That's what happens in church: We come to be taught and instructed in the Word of God and to see God's hand at work in the lives of people.

So how could it be that a whole generation of people could hear the Word and see the hand of God, yet each time they found themselves in trouble, they began to doubt and reject the very God who had delivered them?

There is an often overlooked passage of Scripture that has incredible implications for our present generation. The Bible says, "[God] made known His ways to Moses, / His acts to the children of Israel" (Ps. 103:7 NKJV). These are important words. Moses got to know the ways of God; he was intimately familiar with His strategies, mind-set, and perspective. The children of Israel, on the other hand, got to know only God's acts. This has serious implications for the New Testament believer. We are not to be a people who simply know the *acts* of God, but we are to be a people who know the *ways* of God. Scripture tells us:

"Eye has not seen, nor ear heard,
Nor have entered into the heart of man
The things which God has prepared for those who
    love Him."
But God has revealed them to us through His Spirit.

(1 Cor. 2:9–10 NKJV)

In other words, the Spirit of God, who was not resident within every Old Testament believer but is resident within every New Testament believer, is given to us so that we might come to know the God we serve; not just His acts, but His ways.

Moses knew the ways of God so that in the face of

difficulty, he did not cower or complain. He had received insight into how God works. The children of Israel, however, knowing only the acts of God, were constantly afraid and regularly digressed from their faith, preferring the bondage of Egypt to the liberty of their present and the potential prosperity of their future.

Regretfully, I see a similar attitude in much of the modern-day Church. Our churches are all too often filled with people who have seen the acts of God, but do not know the ways of God. One of the advantages to reading the Old Testament (which amazingly few believers seem to do) is that it reveals the ways and the strategies of God, how He accomplishes great deliverances and how He uses men and women to perform His will. Great insight is available to us in the old covenant regarding the ways of God.

Let me give you an example. I may learn to appreciate, to celebrate, even to be very thankful to someone who time and again has gotten me out of a jam, but that does not mean that I will truly trust that individual. It was the children of Israel's inability to trust God that caused them to be disqualified from receiving their inheritance. When the going got tough, they stalled. Their faith short-circuited because they did not understand that the God they served often put them in

difficult circumstances, surrounded them with enemies, and then encouraged and expected them to trust
Him in the midst of it all. This is one of God's strategies. Trust can be developed only through the knowledge you gain when you actually get to know
someone.

It is this deficiency in the children of Israel that
caused them to cower when they saw the sons of Anak
and the giants in the land of Canaan. They therefore
never crossed into their inheritance (Num. 13–14).
God is looking for a generation of people who not only
know His acts, but who understand His ways and can
trust Him in the midst of difficult and challenging circumstances. It is one thing to be saved; it is quite
another to trust God so much that when everything
looks like it's going to hell, something rises up inside us
and says, "The God who has delivered me will yet
deliver me and shall deliver me again."

God is not looking for a Church full of people who
have come to altars and repented of their sins. He is
looking for a House full of people who will trust and
believe Him and who have learned how to walk out
their faith, even in the midst of opposition.

If there is a restlessness that I sense within the Spirit
of God with the modern-day Church, it is this. We are
a generation of people who have seen and heard more

about God, yet actually know less of God intimately, than perhaps any generation in Church history. It is for this reason that God will sometimes skip one generation, although He loves them dearly, and raise up another generation that will trust and serve Him because they are made of the right stuff.

There is something about people who have been through hell and high water: They have the ability to believe that things are going to work out on their behalf. They wear a confidence that says, "If the enemy could have taken me out, he would have taken me out already." They understand that the very thing that others think should disqualify them is actually the thing that qualifies them for being at the forefront of the move of God.

God is looking for people who know how to go through something and will still trust Him. Many times it's not what you've been through that qualifies or disqualifies you, but it's the fact that you made it through that heightens your usability in the Kingdom of God.

In Numbers 14, we find a generation who have seen the power of God and have been saved with a mighty hand, but have not learned to trust Him. Time and again the people of Israel murmured in the wilderness. When Pharaoh approached, they looked at Moses and said, "Did you bring us out of Egypt to kill us out here?" And Moses replied, "Stand still and see the sal-vation of the Lord." And God saved them. When they got hungry in the wilderness, they looked at Moses and said, "Oh, that we had leeks and onions like back in Egypt," and Moses responded, "God is going to make a way." And God fed them with meat and manna day after day. When they became thirsty in the wilderness, they said, "We're about to die of thirst, Moses," and Moses said, "The God who delivered you, and the God who fed you, will He not also give you water?" And he spoke to a rock, and water flowed out of the rock!

I believe that this first generation of deliverance of the children of Israel is somewhat representative of the generation that is sitting in church pews today. They are genuinely saved and washed in the blood, but they have not developed a relationship with God that enables them to trust Him in the trouble that they find in the natural world. Don't get me wrong; I believe that they're going to heaven, but they may get there sooner than you and me because they have not learned how to resist sickness, ward off disease, or rebuke the devil of poverty from their lives.

Jesus came not simply to get you and me to heaven but also to prepare us to live victoriously on the earth. He wants us to know how to walk in power and how to rebuke the enemy of our souls. He wants us to know how to get water out of a rock, to receive manna in the wilderness, and to watch enemies get swallowed up in seas that they believe never should have parted in the first place.

Has it ever occurred to you that nothing has ever occurred to God? He knows everything. He is never worried, never afraid, never concerned, and nothing ever takes Him by surprise. If we are to be the sons and daughters of God, we must develop that kind of character. (Like you, I am still perfecting it!) We must have the ability to look at our mountains and say, "One of us has got to move, and it ain't gonna be me!"

Although this generation has been in church, they have not learned how to use good warfare. They have settled for being benchwarming Christians and no longer aspire to be first-string players. When God challenges them to possess the land, they are fearful and bring back an evil report, saying, "We cannot do it." God decrees judgment upon this generation for their unbelief. He says to them in essence, "You are delivered, but you have not yet come to know Me. You are free, but you have not learned how to walk by faith or how to stand in the midst of adversity."

The people of Israel said among themselves, "God is going to let us die here." So He looked at them and said, "Just as you have spoken in My hearing, so I will do to you" (Num. 14:28 NKJV). He said, "You said that I'm going to let you die in the wilderness, so I'm going to let you die in the wilderness." We would be wise to watch what we say when we're in trouble! Jesus said, "By your words you will be justified, and by your words you will be condemned" (Matt. 12:37 NKJV); Scripture also says, "The mouth of the upright shall deliver them" (Prov. 12:6 KJV).

Again, God said, "Just as you have spoken in My hearing, so I will do to you: The carcasses of you who have complained against Me shall fall in this wilderness, all of you who were numbered, according to your entire number, from twenty years old and above" (Num. 14:28–29 NKJV). This is an interesting dealing. Here God pronounced judgment on a generation because of its refusal to trust Him in the midst of adversity. This shows us that the God we serve will at times remove His hand from one generation, then place it upon another generation and continue with His plan. At times He chooses a generation simply because He sees in it the raw ingredients that will manifest His Kingdom purpose.

In Numbers 13–14, the Bible says that when the men that Moses sent out to spy out the land of Canaan came back, ten of them gave an evil report. Joshua and Caleb, however, gave a good report, saying in essence,

"We're able to take this land, let's go for it!" So even though they were of the condemned generation, God preserved Caleb and Joshua and promised they would see the land of milk and honey. Here are two men who, because they had the right spirit, the right perspective, and the right attitude, were included in the blessing, regardless of their chronological ages.

Perhaps some of you think that you are excluded from the X Blessing, or this next thing that God is going to do, because of your age. I announce to you in the name of Jesus Christ, if you have the spirit of a warrior, you're in. If you have the spirit to walk by faith, you're in. If you believe when other people seemingly can't, if you praise when other people are crying, and if you go to war when other people worry, you're in. No matter what your age, color, denomination, or hometown, if you're a part of the remnant that says, "Yes, I can, and yes, God will," you're in.

The Word continues: "But your little ones, whom you said would be victims, I will bring in, and they shall know the land which you have despised" (Num. 14:31 NKJV).

Now, the word *known* in this verse is the Hebrew word *yada,* which means "to be intimately acquainted with," and in this scenario refers not only to the land, but with how to possess or actually take hold of the land. God is saying, in essence, that this is something the older generation had refused to learn. This verse is as powerful today as when it was spoken, for there are those in our day who have declared that today's generation will not amount to anything. They have been labeled as dazed, confused, and as victims without the "right stuff."

God says, "The ones whom you have declared would be victims are the very ones that I am going to bless." In the modern context, He says, "The ones that you were so worried about because they were out in the world partying, drug dealing, and clubbing, these are the ones I am going to use." The Bible says, "Man looks at the outward appearance, but the LORD looks at the heart" (1 Sam. 16:7 NKJV).

In Numbers 14, we have the recorded history of God pronouncing judgment upon one generation and blessing upon the other. We have the decree of God over a generation of people who had seen Moses come against the mightiest kingdom on the face of the earth with nothing but a word in his mouth and a stick in his hand. The children of Israel had seen God work miracle after miracle, yet they had not grown enough in their faith to believe God in the midst of adversity. When they got into the wilderness, no sooner did they hear Pharaoh's chariots coming after them than they said,

"Moses! What have you done? Did you bring us out of Egypt to let us die? It would have been better for us back in Egypt."

These are people whom God had delivered, but their deliverance had not yet converted into a lifestyle of trust or faith. They represent a generation of people today who go to church and are saved, but who refuse to walk by faith and continue to murmur when they face adversity. God is not after a group of church-sitting people. He wants men and women, boys and girls who know how to walk by faith and war a good warfare.

Numbers 14:31 refers to Israel's "little ones, whom you said would be victims." In the modern context, one generation of believers is looking at another generation of believers and saying, "These are going to be victims because they don't have the right kind of stuff." One generation has been in church for forty years, but they have been in wilderness church, not Promised Land church. Its members are a complaining, groaning, self-righteous, religious generation and God says, "I'm about to raise up a whole new breed. The very people that you forty-year-church-goin' folk are looking at and saying, 'They're going to be victims,' I say, 'Just watch what I'm going to do with them. I am going to bring them in to possess the land that you have despised, and many of you are going to be scratching your heads and wondering what just happened here!'"

This is the God who flips grace, the God who switches anointings and gives the unexpected the power to do the extraordinary. One of the things that I have been impressed of by the Spirit of God is that He has carefully looked at the heart of today's generation. From His vantage point He sees people who are willing to stay out all night doing something that they believe in. Even if they're dealing drugs and partying now, in them God sees a generation willing to do what they believe in, even if the law tells them it is illegal. These are the kind of people that God is looking for.

I believe that God is going to change the nature of this generation. If we will only bring them to Him, He will bless them and transform their character. They will serve Him and experience great success.

Perhaps you have been looking at this generation and thinking, *Certainly God cannot use this club-going, crack-selling', gang-bangin' generation.* God says, "I've been looking for a generation like this. You may say, "God can't use gang-bangers; they're good for nothing." But He says, "I've been looking for a people who understand covenant." Gang members definitely understand loyalty and relationship. They won't turn each other in, nor will they turn on one another. They will cover one another when they get in trouble. Wouldn't it be wonderful if that were the testimony of the Kingdom of God!

Of this generation, born, schooled, and equipped in Egypt, God says, "I'm about to use them. I'm calling them just as Israel called Joseph's sons born in Egypt, and I'm prepared to bless them with My covenant blessing. I'm about to use them and take them into the land that many people who have been going to church for many years have never seen. I'm about to lay My hands upon people you thought should never have hands laid on them."

12

a remnant church

As long as I can remember, I have tried to be an ardent student of Church history. I have always had a great interest in the architecture of revival. I have read the book of Acts time and again; I love this exposition of the birth and genesis of the Church, how it was born in power and strength and endowed with supernatural anointing.

I remember reading a portion of Acts one day and being struck by the observation that my generation had not experienced much of what was recorded in those pages. That disturbed me, because as I read my Bible, I understand that the Church is not supposed to diminish in power year after year, but grow. I made up my mind that my generation was going to see the power of God that I read about in Acts.

I was tired of reading about revival and of people

being healed as Peter's shadow crossed over them. I was weary of the stories about the miracles of Paul, Stephen, and Philip and about people being raised from the dead. I was impatient to hear yet again about the Welsh Revival in Great Britain or the Azusa Street Revival in Los Angeles. I could no longer just read about men like Charles Finney, Evan Roberts, Charles Wesley, and George Whitefield—men who birthed great revivals and moves of God. I declared to the Lord, "You say that You are the same yesterday, today, and forever, and I believe You. Therefore, I expect You to do a work amongst my generation that surpasses what You did through those who have gone before me. I am not going to die until I see a move of God like what I have read about."

My cry was like that of David: "O God, do not forsake me, / Until I declare Your strength to this generation, / Your power to everyone who is to come" (Ps. 71:18 NKJV).

There is a mentality in the modern-day Church that must be destroyed. It suggests that the power of God was manifested in days of old through people adorned with halos and wings. This present generation of believers numbingly assumes that the people who initiated biblical events and great revivals were somehow spiritually superior to ourselves. That just is not true. The Bible dispels this kind of mythology, for example, in the book of James: "Elijah was a man with a nature *like ours,* and he prayed earnestly that it would not rain; and it did not rain on the land for three years and six months" (James 5:17 NKJV, emphasis mine).

In other words, supernatural beings or winged entities did not perform miracles. Miracles were the product of men and women of God who obeyed the Spirit and believed that God was able to do in their day what He had done in days past.

I believe God is declaring to His present-day Church that there is nothing that we read about, nothing that we have seen, nothing that our great-grandparents have told us about that is impossible for us to manifest ourselves. All we need to do is get into proper position in relationship with God. The generation in which we now live, as degraded and depraved as it is, is one that God desires to use, and He has given us the responsibility and a mandate to call this group of people that much of the Church has turned its back on—young men and women who are wearing their pants baggy and their hats backward because they don't know which direction they're headed. God says, "If you will call them, I'll straighten them up and bring them forward. They're going to be anointed of the Holy Spirit."

Therefore, I am a man on a mission. God has determined to use this generation, which appears to be without direction or purpose, to give birth to the greatest revival and manifestation of God's power that the world has ever seen.

They are the children of Egypt. They were not raised in the Church. They didn't go to Sunday school or Vacation Bible School. They never learned the Ten Commandments or how to quote Scripture. They haven't been to seminary, and they don't have ordination papers. Nobody has laid their hands upon them and blessed them.

But today God is raising up a remnant church, a group of people distinctly different from organized religion and what it has produced. When I speak of the remnant church, I am referring in essence to that group of people within the organized religious institution called Church, who are hearing the voice of the Spirit of God in the "now." They are pursuing God with an abandon toward a fulfillment of destiny.

Not everybody who goes to church is a part of this remnant church. These are people who have been born in Egypt, not in Israel. They have been born and raised outside of the Church. They are coming with definite gifts and callings and exceptional talents and anointings. They're not trying to jockey for anybody's position; they are most definitely not trying to be what religious people think they ought to be. We'd better get ready for this, because God is about to take sons and daughters who have been born and equipped, gifted and anointed in the world, and bring them into the house and treat them as His own.

There is a Church that has been thought dead by people in the world. It is an institution perceived by many to be ineffective, irrelevant, without leadership or strength, but God is raising up a whole new breed of visionary believers who have been divinely positioned to bring the influence of the Kingdom of God. It is imperative that we get this because we are part of this remnant, and we need to understand who we are and what time it is.

More than a decade ago the Spirit of God said to me, "Son, I've put you right in the midst of two generations. You're going to reach the traditional and you're going to reach the untraditional." I am a man in his early thirties who was born to a father in his sixties and was raised with the mentality of an older generation. Most people who have a dad the same age as mine are in their fifties or sixties today. While I was raised with an understanding of that older generation, I was also raised a part of my own generation. I had to depart from the way of my father in order to find God for my generation. He is the same God, but He uniquely reveals Himself to every generation.

The Bible says that King David "served his own generation by the will of God" (Acts 13:36 NKJV). One of the greatest things that can be said about a man or woman of God is that "they served their generation." We must serve our generation by the will of God. I believe that one of the greatest outpourings that we could possibly see in this hour would be a stripping away of the blindness that religion has put upon the Church. I am convinced that this will initiate an awakening unlike anything we've seen throughout our secular society.

Previously I articulated the fact that there is a baptism of repentance being released upon the Church today. Again, that baptism is a supernatural ability given by the Holy Spirit to those who will hear the Word of God and receive it, enabling them beyond their human ability to release old ideas and move forward into the next thing that God is doing. To be effective, we must have to have a change of heart and a change of mind. We cannot reap the harvest with our current mentality.

For this purpose, God is releasing a prophetic anointing upon His Church. This is the visitation that I am looking for—where entire churches that are steeped in religion and tradition (regardless of denominational persuasion) will come to a broader understanding of the body of Christ and the Kingdom of God. We will begin to work together rather than compete with one another. And I promise you, that will get the world's attention.

13

it's happening everywhere

While our primary focus thus far has been upon North America, it is important to recognize that the truths and revelation of the X Blessing transcend culture, ethnicity, and nationality. As we enter this new millennium, we are wise to consider the international implications for the X Blessing.

Around the globe, countries, cities, communities, and even individuals are grasping to redefine the world in which they live. Never has humanity experienced such rapid or confusing change on an international scope. Under the uncertain shadow surrounding this new millennium, people are seeking security. In the midst of bewildering change, people habitually reach for what is familiar. An unfortunate paradox of extreme times is that they often breed conservatism. People entrench rather than expand, and that is not good news for the body of Christ, which tends to favor the confines and dead ends of religion to the cutting edge of Kingdom living and exploration.

Globally we are living in the midst of an unprecedented youth explosion. One-third of the world is under age fifteen, and more than 60 percent of all people living between Los Angeles and the southern tip of South America are under the age of twenty. The average age in Mexico City, the world's largest city at 25 million people, is now fourteen. Regional statistics from the continents of Africa and Asia reveal the same youth trends. Today the majority of the six billion people who inhabit earth are under the age of twenty.[1]

If we are to successfully fulfill the mandate of reaching our generation with the gospel of the kingdom, we must recognize that a primary target is our youth. Any church, ministry, denomination, business, or enterprise that does not recognize this audience is in jeopardy of becoming irrelevant and tragically ineffective.

Recently we were invited to minister in the South American nation of Brazil. We participated in an outdoor festival and crusade in São Paulo, where more than fifteen thousand young people gathered. There is a revolution afoot among the youth of Brazil. They have no interest in religion and they're fed up with impotent, irrelevant churches; however, they quickly recognize authentic Christianity and are calling for an unprecedented move of God across their nation. It was extraordinary to watch fifteen thousand young people jump, head-bang, and dance to the music of this generation. But most compelling was to experience the power and anointing of the Word of the Lord upon a stadium filled with young men and women.

In recent years political scandal, rampant unemployment, and runaway inflation have gripped and crippled Brazil. By the Spirit of the Lord, though, we prophesied and declared, "There is a spiritual uprising being birthed in this nation. There is a turning of the tide. The prisons of religion and tradition are being thrown off, and new liberty is coming in the Spirit to the church in Brazil. I believe that you are part of a new spiritual uprising that God has purposed for this generation for the salvation of the nation. You are more important to God than you realize. The answer to your personal needs, the solutions to your nation's economic and political problems, are in *your* hands. *You* are the people who are to bring a solution. *You* are the only ones who can. For in *you* dwells the Spirit of God, and every answer that your nation needs is in the Spirit of God that resides in *you*."

The Holy Spirit swept across the stadium, ministering to thousands of youth at the same time. Most had their arms stretched to heaven in a posture of absolute surrender and worship. Some were on their knees, and many were in tears as they dedicated their lives and futures to the work of Jesus Christ. I have genuine hope for the future of Brazil. God has His eye upon a new generation that is positioning itself to hear His voice and to obey His directives.

As a local church, the Lord has given us a mandate to take the *whole* gospel to the *whole* world for the sake of mankind's *whole* deliverance. While our Harvest Fire Crusades & Media outreach has significant impact internationally, we are particularly focused upon the continent of Europe. Home to more than 600 million people, only 5 percent of Europeans regularly attend any kind of church, and of those, a much smaller percentage are actually in relationship with Jesus Christ. In recent months we have begun airing our Harvest Fire television broadcasts across Europe.

Amazingly, those who have provided some of the most timely assistance are those who appear the least likely. An entity that has paved the way for broader Christian programming throughout Europe has been the French telecommunications industry. This is extraordinary when one considers that France is one of the most spiritually dark nations on the continent. Today there are more practicing witches and warlocks in the city of Paris than there are evangelical pastors; however, we are living in a season where God is choosing the unexpected through which to manifest His plans and purpose.

The majority of the world's people now live in cities, and one of the world's truly great metropolitan centers is London. London is a puzzle of never-ending contradiction. It is a world-class city energized by a vibrant and highly visible youth culture, yet held captive by its history and tradition. It is a metropolitan center gripped by a cynical spirit, yet so hopeful and in search of what is authentic. It is a city rich in innovation, yet riddled with decay. It is truly international, yet unceasingly British.

The youth of this city are ripe for revival and hunger for that which is genuine. They have little time for anything based solely upon tradition or ceremony, especially church. In contrast, they are very open to those who demonstrate both the power and relevance of God. They are the first to tell you that they will never "play church," but that they earnestly want to know God. Those who are believers sincerely want renewal within their churches, and they're hungry for the relevant and on-time Word. They respond with great passion and earnestness to anointed worship.

We are excited about ongoing relationships and

ministry opportunities with the youth of this strategic city. Throughout London and all of Great Britain is an entire generation of people who are not yet connected with Christ. Ian was one of these.

Ian is eighteen years old and lives in the Smithfield District near the University of London. Often loud, regularly disrespectful, and seemingly out of control, Ian could be representative of almost any youth from an inner-city neighborhood. Ian left school at age sixteen and, until recently, his life revolved around neighborhood football matches and drinking binges with his "mates." Technically unqualified for most jobs, he opts instead to receive a small but regular unemployment check.

Throughout London are a growing number of youth like Ian; they are neighborhood kids who have "checked out" and now simply hang out. While they are not content with what they've got, most cannot believe they will get anything better. These are not the young people lined up outside of clubs in Soho or packed into trendy West End cafes; these kids rarely leave the confines of their neighborhoods. Unlike American gangs, they have no names, no codes, and they wear no colors, but they are fiercely territorial of their run-down environs; for some it's all that they have.

These groups exhibit an extraordinary loyalty

among themselves. Many have learned to drink by the time they're age seven or eight, and by eighteen they're bona fide alcoholics. Their parents are either nonexistent or long ago gave up on their kids. Ian's father disappeared a decade ago; his mother has battled her own drug and alcohol issues and shows up at home "when she can." Ian was infamous for causing confusion and had developed an aggravating ability for manipulating any conversation—it was his way of being "in control." But Ian was radically transformed when he met Jesus Christ.

A local London youth group adopted Ian's neighborhood to pray for and to ask the Lord to use as an example of His love and redemption. Ian and his friends initially terrorized these young urban missionaries, but they didn't give up. They gathered every morning, Monday through Friday, and prayed for the neighborhood and for the kids they met. They believed the Lord would invade these empty lives and work supernaturally. They built skateboard ramps for the neighborhood, held concerts, provided a computer training center, and simply hung out with those who would talk with them.

Ian was cruel and beyond skeptical at first. He knew the "do-gooders" wouldn't last; they never did. His boys were known for being violent, and they were going to give these "religious brats" a reason to leave. But the youth group kept coming back. Every Friday night they opened the church and provided a place for the neighborhood youth to hang out. It took weeks before any of them ventured inside the building, but once they did, they kept coming back. Instinctively they knew that they'd found a safe place.

Ian's life was radically impacted when he listened to one of the boys from the youth group tell about his love for Jesus Christ. Amazingly, this guy looked like Ian. His hair was buzzed, and he wore strategically placed earrings and clothes that Ian could relate to. He talked about football and music and, like Ian, he'd been a "'hood rat" in another part of London. Ian couldn't believe that God would really live in a guy like this, but he listened anyway.

The boy talked about Jesus being God's Son and having lived on earth. He spoke about the cross and Jesus' death and resurrection and about eternal life. It wasn't theologically deep, but it was accurate. Ian couldn't shake portions of the conversation from his mind. Not long after, Ian prayed to receive Jesus Christ as his Lord and Savior, and, being the leader that he is, he promptly brought some of his friends to hear about Jesus. Together they're learning that it is possible to step out of their dead-end world into a future filled with promise. These liberally pierced young men are relentless in telling others about Christ; their newfound love is infectious.

London, like most world-class cities, is packed with young people just like Ian. Government schemes, social welfare programs, boys and girls clubs are not going to touch these kids. They cannot provide the answers or resources this population needs. Time and again the "Ians" are told what they cannot do. It's time we start telling young people like Ian what they *can* do: They *can* be accepted as they are. They *can* live lives of purpose and destiny. They *can* find meaningful service and employment. They *can* find trustworthy friendships and relationships. They *can* remove themselves from the pain and disappointments of their pasts. They *can* be free from drugs. They *can* be hopeful for their futures. As the Church we have the answer for them in the person of Jesus Christ.

God's promise that He has His eye upon this generation is true not only for those living in San Francisco, Philadelphia, Atlanta, or Boston; it is true for the residents of London, Nairobi, Buenos Aires, and Singapore. His purpose isn't limited to a location or to a particular nation. We are living within a dispensation of time where God is flipping His established order to release a seed of deliverance that will enable unprecedented numbers of people to enter into relationship with the Lord Jesus Christ.

I am absolutely convinced that God is doing His greatest work in our day and that we have not yet begun to see all He will do as we follow Him with our whole heart. God has His eye upon Generation X. He is choosing the unexpected to transform cities and to shake nations. The potential for today's generation throughout North America and around the world is limitless.

14

the field is the world

as I've said before, the Spirit of God is releasing upon His Church an anointing to rethink, reassess, and reevaluate those things that we have long held sacred and assumed to be true. He is beginning to literally transform the perspectives of some of His people about the Church and the Kingdom of God so that we can effectively reap the harvest in this last day. This anointing, which I have called the baptism of repentance, allows us to remove the glasses of religion that have obscured the Church's vision so we can take a raw look at the rule of God as it comes.

In order for the Church to be effective in the complex world in which we live, we must go through a metamorphosis. We cannot reap the harvest being given to us without a vast transformation in our current mentality. The harvest simply is too big to accommodate that. We desperately need a change of mind, a change of heart, and a change of perspective away from traditional, religious, and ceremonial vantage points that will enable us to come into a more comprehensive understanding of the Kingdom of God.

It is worthy to note that Jesus did not speak much about the Church but said volumes about the Kingdom of God. I contend that if you really read and follow the ministry of Jesus, you will see that He did not come to establish a church, but a kingdom; and the Kingdom of God is far bigger than the Church.

I understand that that statement is somewhat revolutionary. Most people equate the Church with the Kingdom of God, but when you look at what Jesus said, you will find that the modern Church not only falls far short of a proper representation of it but could not possibly encompass it.

The Kingdom of God is not a place. Heaven and earth are places, but the Kingdom of God is not. Jesus made this point clear in Luke 17, when the Pharisees asked when the Kingdom of God would come. He said, "The kingdom of God does not come with observation; nor will they say, 'See here!' or 'See there!' For indeed, the kingdom of God is within you" (Luke 17:20–21 NKJV).

Listen to those words. Jesus said that the Kingdom of God does not come with *observation;* in other words, you will not be able to see it by merely looking. Nor will you be able to say, "The Kingdom is over here," or "The Kingdom is over there," for the Kingdom of God resides "within you."

The Kingdom of God is a perspective, a position, and an attitude that result from the power of God that resides within us after we have received the Lord Jesus Christ. As we saw in a previous chapter, the word *kingdom* comes from the Greek word *basileia*, which translates "the rule of God, the realm of God and the royalty or reign of God."[1] So when Jesus declares that the Kingdom is coming, He is talking about the rule of God coming and God's realm infiltrating the world in which we live. The Kingdom of God is the rule of God in our lives by which He causes us, by the power of His Spirit, to make decisions that produce righteousness, or right standing with God.

The Kingdom of God differs from the Church in that the Church is to be a gathering of Kingdom people. We would be wise to understand that all of God's Kingdom people are not going to fit into our paradigm of the organized Church and its ministries. Let me give you an example from the Old Testament. Under the old covenant, the Israelites set up the tabernacle of Moses in the midst of the camp. The Aaronic and Levitical priesthood was responsible to keep the tabernacle functioning (maintain the altars, oversee the sacrifices).

Only the priests were allowed inside the tabernacle. That did not mean that the people outside of the tabernacle were no longer Israelites. They were the people of God; they simply did not have the role of maintaining the tabernacle. If you apply that paradigm to the modern-day Church, you can understand that there are people outside the tabernacle who belong just as much to Israel or to the modern-day Church as those of us who are "priests"—who have the responsibility of keeping the church fires burning on a weekly basis. The Church is a gathering of Kingdom people, but not all of God's Kingdom people are necessarily going to be reflected in or through the realms of organized religion and church.

Jesus told His disciples a parable:

> The kingdom of heaven is like a man who sowed good seed in his field; but while men slept, his enemy came and sowed tares among the wheat and went his way.

> But when the grain had sprouted and produced a crop, then the tares also appeared.

So the servants of the owner came and said to him, "Sir, did you not sow good seed in your field? How then does it have tares?"

He said to them, "An enemy has done this." The servants said to him, "Do you want us then to go and gather them up?"

But he said, "No, lest while you gather up the tares you also uproot the wheat with them.

"Let both grow together until the harvest, and at the time of harvest I will say to the reapers, 'First gather together the tares and bind them in bundles to burn them, but gather the wheat into my barn.'"

(Matt. 13:24–30 NKJV)

The disciples asked Jesus to explain the parable, so He said:

He who sows the good seed is the Son of Man. The field is the world, the good seeds are the sons of the kingdom, but the tares are the sons of the wicked one. The enemy who sowed them is the devil, the harvest is the end of the age, and the reapers are the angels.

(Matt. 13:37–39 NKJV)

Notice that Jesus provided a line-by-line interpretation of this parable. I submit to you that this is not just another parable about the second coming of Christ, although many have misconstrued it to be so. I believe that it is about what God is doing in and through His Church before Jesus comes again, and it is central to understanding the importance of the X Blessing and God's purpose in calling forth this generation. I am convinced that we have incompletely interpreted this parable to mean that the field is the Church. Jesus clearly stated that "the field is the *world*." This parable is not about what *is happening* in the Church but about what God purposes *to happen* through the Church in the world. The field is the world. Jesus did not come to establish a Church; He came to establish a Kingdom. Beloved, there is a world of difference. Children of the Church know how to conduct themselves in church; children of the Kingdom know how to conduct themselves in the world.

The Word reads, "The kingdom of heaven is like a man who sowed good seed in his field" (Matt. 13:24 NKJV). In this parable the sower is the Son of Man

(Jesus), and the good seed are the children of the Kingdom. We can accurately say, then, that the Son of Man (Jesus) sows good seed (children of the Kingdom) into His field (the world).

It is children of the Kingdom that He desires to be sown into the world. That alone is a different understanding from what much of the modern-day Church holds. Many people believe that the Church is God's field and the world belongs to the enemy, but God says the world is the field. It is not Jesus' aim to sow people into the Church—He wants to sow people into the world. Specifically, He wants to sow children of the Kingdom into the world. Because our perspective and doctrine have been Church oriented and not Kingdom oriented, through our preaching and instruction we have produced children of the Church rather than children of the Kingdom.

Unfortunately, I am not sure that we have enough children of the Kingdom yet to influence all the areas of the world that God really wants us to influence. Our doctrine has produced a generation of people with a church mentality. We have taught people how to be children of the Church, but when you take them outside their church, suddenly they do not know how to conduct themselves. The goal of the Kingdom is not for people to come into the Church and to hide out and feel safe and never leave. The idea is for people to be saved and then instructed in the ways of the Kingdom of God in the gathering of the Church. As children of the Kingdom gather, they become the Church and they are instructed and empowered to take that perspective, fragrance, and authority of the Kingdom of God with them wherever they go.

Let me qualify the word *world*. The Greek word for *world* is the word *cosmos,* which means "the arrangement, decorations, props, or the order of things."[2] Because I live in Southern California, in the center of the entertainment industry, I have a vivid perspective on what props and decorations are. Most of the movies and sitcoms that we see on television are shot in studios and on sets. The tables, couches, chairs, refrigerators, and other items that look real are simply props on a stage. You and I must understand that the visible world—the order of things in which we live—is not the order of things that God originally purposed. If it was, why would Jesus have told us to pray, "Thy kingdom come" (Matt. 6:10 KJV), which means, "Your order come, Your rule come—Thy will be done in earth as it is in heaven"? Obviously it is not being done in the earth, or we would not have to pray for it.

Child of God, one of the primary reasons that you and I have been saved and left here on the planet is so

that God can fill us with His Word and with His Spirit
and sow us into the present arrangement or systems of
the world that have no redeeming atmosphere or qual-
ity. We are mandated to be salt and light to the world,
which means we are to serve as preservative and flavor
as well as illumination to the planet. As children of the
Kingdom we are to be in every realm and every
endeavor declaring the Kingdom of God. God wants to
sow children of the Kingdom into the television industry and into every realm of education. He wants children who understand His Kingdom authority,
empowerment, and perspective permeating the arts,
politics, business, and music. God desires men and
women, filled with His mind, heart, Spirit, and perspective to revolutionize the sports and entertainment industries. God wants children of the Kingdom everywhere
taking territory from the devil, but He wants us to go
forth with a Kingdom understanding and perspective.

It is no wonder that much of today's generation
finds the Church to be irrelevant. After all, much of the
Church would never show up where most of this generation lives. A church that is blinded and held hostage
by religious devils wouldn't be caught dead in a club,
at a hip-hop concert, or in a music or television studio.
Such people would be reluctant to interact with someone whose business is "running the streets."

They don't understand that participating in the Kingdom of God means doing more than wearing a faded "His Pain, Your Gain" T-shirt or displaying "Honk If You Love Jesus" bumper stickers on their cars! The Kingdom of God has nothing to do with pancake breakfasts or Friday-night bingo. The Kingdom of God is not stained-glass windows or church buildings.

The Kingdom of God is to invade this world and its systems and turn them upside down—to redeem industries and transform enterprise with the perspective of eternity. When the Kingdom of God comes, it will expose counterfeit kingdoms and restore that which is authentic. It will reestablish the order of heaven throughout the earth.

I admit this calls for a radical adjustment of mind, attitude, and perspective. It is revolutionary. The Kingdom of God is not about taking the best and strongest gifts out of the world; it's about calling them, blessing them, anointing them, and sowing them back into the world to transform and to change it.

The parable of the sower further instructs that tares (weeds) were sown among the wheat while men slept. Could it be that much of the Church has been sleeping, or in actuality has been unconscious, while our enemy is sowing weeds among the wheat? I'm afraid that much of the Church has been sleeping for several generations. We've pulled out because we have not had the mentality of the Kingdom of God. God wants to fill us so full of His Word and His Spirit that we are not afraid to take up residence in the world and to reestablish ownership and to take our proper place of dominion and authority in the world.

We can see through the parable that the good seed represents children of the Kingdom. Unlike some of my colleagues, however, I do not necessarily believe that the tares or weeds represent sinners. Notice that Scripture says that the tares are sown among the wheat, or among the product or the fruit of the children of the Kingdom. Therefore, they must resemble them closely enough to dwell among them. I believe that the tares represent those who have come to the altar and have given their hearts to Christ, but have not grown in the knowledge of the Kingdom of God. They are saved but have not had their minds transformed or renewed through the Word of God and the truths of the Kingdom. These are churchgoing people who still operate with carnal attitudes and a secular mentality; they are driven by their passions and their flesh rather than by the mind of the Spirit of God. They are children of the Church, rather than children of the Kingdom.

The enemy takes these repentant but untransformed believers and sows them in among the wheat, who are the true children of the Kingdom. Side by side, they look alike. They are people who know just enough about church to be dangerous and to fool the world into thinking that they have the mind-set that represents the Kingdom of God. Unfortunately, many of these people misrepresent our God and His Kingdom to people who earnestly seek an answer.

I submit to you that God is raising up in this last hour true children of the Kingdom, and He's putting them on prime time. If we follow the leading of the Spirit of God, He is going to provide us in this generation with avenues of communication and the world is going to see the real children of the Kingdom of God come forth.

The Spirit of God is conducting a supernatural uncovering and crying out, "Will the real children of the Kingdom please stand up?" In this hour, in our generation, children of the Kingdom are being positioned and established in strategic areas of influence in entertainment, politics, sports, government, health care, and every other significant arena.

Some of you reading these pages right now have a dream in your heart, something that has been placed there by the Spirit of God, and religious-minded people have said to you, "You can't do that and be a Christian; you can't go there and be a Christian; you can't be this and be a Christian." But I submit to you that if you go to influence with the perspective of the power and the Kingdom of God, that the vision in your spirit is very possibly what God would have you do.

There are industries, markets, and populations throughout the world that we cannot touch, let alone infiltrate and reclaim, without Generation X. They have been uniquely equipped with the tools, talents, abilities, and dreams to go back to Egypt and influence it for the glory of God. As the Church, we have a job to do, and we cannot possibly fulfill it without them. As a matter of fact, we're not meant to. We are mandated to do it together.

I want to see young men and women who are saved to the bone and filled with the power of the Holy Spirit embedded within the heart of advertising, leading the way in setting trends and communicating to the masses. It is time that we have more godly representatives of Generation X influencing all areas of the music industry, including the Hip-hop Nation. Our children need godly role models on the court and on the big screen, and this marked generation should lead the way. Mechanics, nurses, computer specialists, artists, social workers, attorneys—all these occupations and more should be experiencing the divine upheaval of the coming of the children of the Kingdom. I believe that in this hour God is sowing His children of the Kingdom into these industries according to His own will.

One final observation: the Bible says in this parable that when the tares were discovered among the wheat, some of Jesus' overzealous disciples asked if they should separate them. Jesus forthrightly said, "No . . . let both grow together until the harvest, and at the time of harvest I will say to the reapers, 'First gather together the tares and bind them in bundles to burn them, but gather the wheat into my barn'" (Matt. 13:29–30 NKJV).

For some time people have heralded the idea that we are living in the great day of harvest. If that is true, and I believe that it is, I submit to you that before sinners are harvested into the Church, there must be a harvest of church people into the Kingdom of God. In the time of harvest, God will begin to separate children of the Church from children of the Kingdom.

Notice what Jesus said as this parable closes: He declared that at the end of the age, the reapers will come and gather all things that offend out of the Kingdom. The word *offend* comes from the Greek word *scandalon,* which means "trap."[3] In other words, in the end time or in the time of harvest, the angels are going to come and remove those things that have trapped people in mind-sets and mentalities of religiosity. I believe that Jesus is going to release the liberated people into the Kingdom of God. For He says, "Then the righteous [or those who are truly in right standing with God] will shine forth as the sun in the kingdom of their Father" (Matt. 13:43 NKJV).

Certainly we will not need to shine like the sun in heaven, for Scripture declares that Jesus is the Light of that city. No, the place where God needs us to shine brightly is here on earth.

Some of you have been feeling a restlessness in your spirit and mind, a dissatisfaction with the status quo, a repulsion of organized Churchanity and religion and yet a passionate and overwhelming love for Jesus Christ. Chances are that you are being equipped to come into the Kingdom and be at the forefront of a glorious, life-changing transformation.

15

a knu generation

generation X is, in many ways, a banner generation positioned to signal victory throughout the world. It is also a symbol of defeat for the enemy because he has lost a generation he thought was his. Of this generation that the devil has warred against, deceived, and attempted to destroy, the Lord says, "They are rescued and safe in Me. I have marked them for release, and not only them; their deliverance is a trigger that will release cities, nations, and continents. Through them I am unveiling an epoch of time, a season of transfer from the expected to the unexpected. They are marked for greatness because they will believe Me. I have marked them to spark revival and renewal, and they are the genesis for the greatest wave of salvation the world has known."

Generation X will no longer be a variable, but a

generation with specific purpose. They will capture the attention of media, government, the arts, and education, and they will demonstrate true Kingdom prosperity. I believe it will be the children and the youth of this nation who will ignite fires of revival through worship. It will be Generation X that will pour the fuel of praise and intensify the fire of the Holy Spirit. Throughout history, some of the most extraordinary moves of God have been accompanied by unusual releases of worship and the supernatural among children and youth.

Here is an example. In one Pacific Northwest community, Eskimos, Klinkets, and Caucasians are coming together for the first time in decades, and the Church is leading the way. At a recent worship service all three ethnic groups gathered in a posture of solidarity and unity. As the service progressed, a five-year-old boy got out of his seat, walked directly to the front of the auditorium, and reached for the microphone, explaining that he had something to say. He turned and faced the congregation and began to prophesy. It was a powerful word directly from the throne of God.

In the midst of his declaration, a woman with a large goiter protruding from her neck caught this young man's attention. With a five-year-old's curiosity, the boy stepped off the platform for a closer look!

"Ooh!" he said. "What's that? Oh, no! Jesus don't want you like that." He reached up, touched her shoulder, and she was slain in the Holy Spirit; the goiter immediately began to shrink. She was down, the goiter was on its way out, and the minister was only five! The young minister returned to the platform, finished delivering the prophetic word, and nonchalantly returned to his seat.

Expect it! That's what time it is! God is choosing to use the unexpected.

The Old Testament book of Judges records the story of the children of Israel preparing for battle against their enemy the Benjamites. Before they went to war, the Israelites sought God's battle plan for victory: "'Which of us shall go up first to battle against the children of Benjamin?' The Lord said, 'Judah first!'" (Judges 20:18 NKJV).

Judah was not the firstborn; he was the fourth son of the patriarch Jacob. As a matter of fact, God intentionally bypassed Judah's three older brothers, who had disqualified themselves because of sin, and chose Judah to lead His people into victory. Judah's name literally means "praise." God didn't send the heavy guns or the mightiest warriors, He sent praise to lead the way.

In Chapter 4 we discovered a generational digression recorded in Proverbs:

There is a generation that curses its father,
And does not bless its mother.
There is a generation that is pure in its own eyes,
Yet is not washed from its filthiness.
There is a generation—oh, how lofty are their eyes!
And their eyelids are lifted up.
There is a generation whose teeth are like swords,
And whose fangs are like knives.

(Prov. 30:11–14 NKJV)

We determined that verse 11 could be representative of the 1960s, verse 12 the 1970s, verse 13 the 1980s, and verse 14 the 1990s.

God chose the fourth son, Judah, to lead the children of Israel (a type and shadow of the Church) into battle and to victory. He chose "praise" to lead His people into victory. Is it possible that the Lord is once again choosing the fourth son—Generation X, the fourth generation—to lead His Church into victory? Is it possible that He has determined to send "praise" first as His battle strategy for this new millennium?

Praise is an extraordinary battle strategy. It is the weapon of choice from heaven. It is the tool that guarantees victory, that allows access to empires and kingdoms, and that signals defeat and breaks the back of the enemy.

True and powerful praise is a weapon. Often it is boisterous and exuberant, much like the youth of our present generation. Powerful praise is generally a result of a deep appreciation and gratitude to God. Scripture instructs that those who are forgiven much, love much. It is not surprising that God would uniquely equip this generation coming out of sin and diabolical attack to offer a powerful, pure, and piercing praise that will shake the kingdoms of darkness to their very foundations.

With many in my congregation coming from this Generation X, I have noticed that when people are saved out of lifestyles of darkness and situations of destruction, they are eager to praise God and are unconcerned about who is watching. They have an authentic and heartfelt appreciation for the God who has delivered them, and they do not forget from whence they have come.

God has given us a mandate to call sons and daughters out of Egypt and into relationship with their covenant Father. We are calling forth a KNU Generation—Kingdom Nation Uniting—a generation pronounced new through music, worship, and the Word of God. We are calling forth by the Spirit of God a generation that I believe will lead the Church into new dimensions of victory, strength, and power.

Throughout North America and other regions of the world, we are targeting strategic metropolitan centers for KNU Generation Miracle Crusades. The specific target group for these crusades are youth and those who have felt disoriented, disenfranchised, or left out and who have found modern religion irrelevant to their lives.

We have been commissioned to call sons and daughters who have been born in Egypt and who have been hiding out in the world into relationship with God. We are to encourage them to bring their gifts, their talents, and their abilities and submit them at the feet of a loving God to be blessed and anointed. Our objective is to call them forth as Israel called Joseph's sons forth to bless them and to say to them, "Whether you realize it or not, you belong to God. Every good and perfect gift comes from the Father of lights, and in Him there is no shadow of turning. What is resident within you, whether you recognize it yet or not, is from God."

We desire to inject into this generation a sense of hope, a sense of purpose, a sense of destiny, and an understanding that God is not holy because He is boring, but God is holy because He is distinct and separate from anything and anyone that they have ever met or experienced. The word *holy* means "to be separate or to be other than." We want to raise up a holy generation through KNU.

From a spiritual perspective, one of the most powerful elements of strength in any generation is understanding the prophetic declaration that has been pronounced over it. According to the book of Acts, through the power and the revelation of the Holy Spirit, Peter stood and said, "This is what was spoken by the prophet Joel: '. . . Your sons and your daughters shall prophesy, / Your young men shall see visions'" (Acts 2:16–17 NKJV). It was here that Peter discovered his place in the prophetic unfolding of God's purpose and destiny for the ages. The Church was birthed and the most powerful move of God, up until that time, was released.

When a generation understands that God has already spoken prophetically over them and discovers that it is possible to find their place in that prophetic unfolding, great power is available. This is why in this hour we stand and declare over this generation that they are not uninspired, unintelligent, shiftless, or a variable. They are God's marked generation for deliverance and revival.

KNU is not a program as much as it is a paradigmatic shift in perspective. It is an alteration and realignment of understanding. It is not a formula for a meeting, nor is it a system or a program that you "work." Rather, it is a perspective about a generation and an understanding of a divine dispensation of time. It is the product of an inspiration, an illumination, and a revelation of the Spirit of God in the heart of a young man: Contrary to the epitaph that has been declared over this present generation, just beneath the clouds of disillusionment, negativity, and dejection lies a yet untapped resource, the strategy of God for a generation. It is the X Blessing, and it is for the X Generation.

notes

CHAPTER 2

1. Geoffrey T. Holtz, *Welcome to the Jungle: The Why Behind "Generation X"* (New York: St. Martin's, 1995), 1.
2. William Strauss et al., *Thirteenth Generation: Abort, Retry, Ignore, Fail?* (New York: Vintage Books, 1993), 7.
3. Holtz, *Welcome to the Jungle*, 4.
4. Strauss, *Thirteenth Generation*, 10.
5. Ibid., 7.
6. Ibid., 18.
7. James Strong, *The New Strong's Exhaustive Concordance of the Bible* (Nashville: Thomas Nelson Publishers, 1990), #932.

CHAPTER 5

1. Strong's, #3340.

2. Strong's, #907.
3. Strong's, #3340.

CHAPTER 13
1. *World Advance*, September/October 1996 (vol. 33, issue 1).

CHAPTER 14
1. Strong's, #932.
2. Strong's, #2889.
3. Strong's, #4625.

about the author

bISHOP CLARENCE E. MCCLENDON is the senior pastor of Church of the Harvest, a rapidly growing multi-ethnic congregation in inner-city Los Angeles with more than twelve thousand people in weekly attendance. Bishop McClendon is a unique young man whose voice has been raised up by God to fan the flames of revival throughout the body of Christ and to bring the message of salvation, coupled with the miraculous healing power of Christ Jesus, to a new generation of people. As a pastor and evangelist, McClendon has traveled extensively, preaching and ministering in healing and miracle services throughout North America and internationally. Raised in Decatur, Illinois, he began preaching at the age of fifteen and assumed his first pastorate at age nineteen.

Bishop McClendon is the founder and president of

Harvest Fire Crusades & Media, Inc. and Kingdom Harvest Ministries, Inc., ministries that encompass weekly international television and radio broadcasts that touch more than 200 million homes worldwide and sponsor national and international ministry crusades. In addition, Bishop McClendon hosts an annual conference that draws thousands of people to Los Angeles each summer.

Currently Bishop McClendon serves on the Bishop's Council of the Full Gospel Baptist Church Fellowship as the Bishop of Fellowship Relations. He also serves as a board member with the *Do Something* Foundation, a think tank of some of America's top young leaders. In 1994, Bishop McClendon received his Doctorate of Divinity from Baptist Christian University International of Orlando, Florida.